NEW MIGRATION REALITIES

About Policy Network

Policy Network is an international think tank and research institute. Its network spans national borders across Europe and the wider world with the aim of promoting the best progressive thinking on the major social and economic challenges of the 21st century.

Our work is driven by a network of politicians, policymakers, business leaders, public service professionals, and academic researchers who work on long-term issues relating to public policy, political economy, social attitudes, governance and international affairs. This is complemented by the expertise and research excellence of Policy Network's international team.

A platform for research and ideas

- Promoting expert ideas and political analysis on the key economic, social and political challenges of our age.
- Disseminating research excellence and relevant knowledge to a wider public audience through interactive policy networks, including interdisciplinary and scholarly collaboration.
- Engaging and informing the public debate about the future of European and global progressive politics.

A network of leaders, policymakers and thinkers

- Building international policy communities comprising individuals and affiliate institutions.
- Providing meeting platforms where the politically active, and potential leaders of the future, can engage with each other across national borders and with the best thinkers who are sympathetic to their broad aims.
- Engaging in external collaboration with partners including higher education institutions, the private sector, thinktanks, charities, community organisations, and trade unions.
- Delivering an innovative events programme combining in-house seminars with large-scale public conferences designed to influence and contribute to key public debates.

www.policy-network.net

About the Barrow Cadbury Fund

The Barrow Cadbury Fund is a Company Limited by Guarantee, set-up by its founders Barrow Cadbury and Geraldine Southall to allow greater flexibility in the couple's giving. The Fund is non charitable and aims to further its mission of bringing about socially just change.

NEW MIGRATION REALITIES

Inclusive Narratives

Maeve Glavey

}{
policy network

ROWMAN &
LITTLEFIELD
————INTERNATIONAL

London • New York

Barrow
Cadbury
Fund

Published by Rowman & Littlefield International Ltd.
Unit A, Whitacre Mews, 26-34 Stannary Street, London, SE11 4AB
www.rowmaninternational.com

Rowman & Littlefield International Ltd.is an affiliate of Rowman & Littlefield
4501 Forbes Boulevard, Suite 200, Lanham, Maryland 20706, USA
With additional offices in Boulder, New York, Toronto (Canada), and
Plymouth (UK)
www.rowman.com

British Library Cataloguing in Publication Data
A catalogue record for this book is available from the British Library

ISBN: PB 978-1-78660-528-3
ISBN: eBook 978-1-78660-529-0

Library of Congress Cataloging-in-Publication Data
Library of Congress Control Number: 2017949587

♾ ™ The paper used in this publication meets the minimum requirements of
American National Standard for Information Sciences—Permanence of Paper for
Printed Library Materials, ANSI/NISO Z39.48-1992.

Printed in the United States of America

CONTENTS

List of Figures   vii

Acknowledgements   ix

Introduction   1

Existing Narratives   9

Attitudes and Concerns about Immigration   33

Case Studies   53

New Narratives   75

Conclusion   93

References   97

LIST OF FIGURES

Figure 2.1   Overall Immigration   35

Figure 2.2   Net Migration   35

Figure 2.3   Asylum applications per 100,000 local population in 2015   36

Figure 2.4   Those identifying immigration as a top issue facing their country   36

Figure 2.5   Those identifying immigration as a top issue facing the EU   37

Figure 2.6   Those identifying immigration as an issue affecting them personally   38

Figure 2.7   Those who think immigration has placed too much pressure on public services in their country   39

Figure 2.8   Immigration is causing my country to change in ways that I don't like (2016)   41

Figure 2.9   Negative feeling towards immigration of people from the EU   42

Figure 2.10   Negative feeling of towards immigration of people from outside the EU   42

Figure 2.11   Fears about refugees (2016)   43

Figure 2.12   Unfavourable view of Muslims in our country (data not available for Sweden in 2006)   44

Figure 2.13   Muslims want to form a distinct group (rather than adopt the customs of wider society) (data not available for Sweden in 2006)   44

Figure 2.14   Those who think the government is doing a poor
              job of managing immigration   49

ACKNOWLEDGEMENTS

A number of people were involved in the design, research and publication of this project. My thanks go to Renaud Thillaye for his careful oversight of the project from its early stages of development, assistance with the research, and insight into the wider political debates in the UK and France in particular. His guidance was invaluable in completing this work. Thank you to Patrick Diamond for his supervision of the project and contribution in particular to developing the policy recommendations, which conclude the publication.

I would also like to thank the wider team at Policy Network for their support with the research and logistics surrounding the project. Thanks in particular to Robert Philpot, Matthew Lloyd and Matthew Laza for their involvement in the editorial process.

The research was made possible by generous support from the Barrow Cadbury Fund. Thank you to Ayesha Saran and Diana Ruthven for working with me throughout the process and for sharing their insight and expertise.

Finally, a sincere thanks to all of those working in the fields of migration and integration across the four focus countries who so generously gave up their time to be interviewed, offer comments, and participate in the events associated with the project. Building better narratives around migration begins with improved communication and it was extremely valuable to meet with so many people of different backgrounds who have dedicated themselves to the understanding of this field.

INTRODUCTION

2016 was by any account an eventful year. The Brexit vote and the election of Donald Trump were characterised by many as the triumph of demagoguery over reason, fiction over fact. A populist tide was apparently sweeping the western world, leaving a trail of chaos and disbelief in its wake, at least for those who didn't vote for it. The crisis seemed to have its roots in dissatisfaction with unresponsive elites, with bottled-up resentment exploding forth as millions of people marched to the polls to vote for change.

Yet, both those seemingly cataclysmic results were exceptionally close calls. Forty-eight per cent of voters in the UK cast their ballot against Brexit and Trump lost the popular vote in the US by a considerable margin, as well as winning fewer Electoral College votes than Barack Obama four years previously. The majority of western democracies are still ruled by governments in which mainstream parties dominate, at least for now. All of this suggests that we are facing a moment of both threat and possibility. Progressives can retreat despondent in the face of the populist challenge, or they can choose to engage and guide the discussion in a more productive direction. Populism is certainly strong, but how the mainstream reacts to the issues it throws up matters greatly. Populism is not an inherently negative force, but poses a challenge that ought to jolt mainstream actors into action, driving them to respond more effectively to public concerns and adapt accordingly. If the right choices are made, existing support for the mainstream can be maintained and lost support regained.

The populist picture in Europe encompasses a range of forces. The populist right frequently focuses on national identity and advocates a return to nationalist values and closed-border policies. The populist left rages against capitalism and appeals to embattled workers dismayed by the impact of austerity on both their own lives and their countries more generally. Mostly, they appear as traditionally structured political parties, but sometimes they take more loosely organised forms, as in the case of the Five Star Movement in Italy. Left-wing populism has frequently found support in southern Europe, while rightwing populism has been more common in northern Europe, driven in part by anger at bailing out what is seen as the continent's profligate south, combined with a deep anxiety brought on by the refugee crisis and terrorist attacks. Supporters do not always divide neatly along traditional political lines and the concerns of left and rightwing populist parties sometimes intersect, finding common ground, for example, in their frequent scepticism towards the EU. What they invariably have in common is a deep sense of dissatisfaction with existing political systems and the available political choices.

If mainstream political forces are to address this sense of frustration and respond to the populist challenge, they need – to echo the phrase used to such powerful effect by the Brexit leave campaign – to 'take back control' of the political conversation. This book is concerned with how that can be done specifically in responding to the case of rightwing populist parties who have increasingly coalesced around one particular trend: opposition to immigration. That is, the inward migration to 'their' countries of foreigners deemed undesirable, whatever their motive for movement. At the heart of this opposition is a narrative which pits the good, patriotic people of the host country against a threatening, foreign 'other'. This is not a story about human commonality or shared aims, but about a competitive, zero-sum game in which resources are scarce, threats are everywhere and when somebody gains, somebody else has to lose. It is one that can and should be challenged by those who believe in economic, social and political progress, and who wish to maintain collaborative approaches at a time when politics is being increasingly defined in terms of open versus closed.

GLOBAL MIGRATION

The problem with the populists' narrative about immigration is that, as with their approach to other issues, it takes a messy, complex, difficult subject, and distils it into simplistic soundbites. Mainstream parties, while guided by different ideologies, have nonetheless been increasingly guilty of similar behaviour. The 2015–2016 refugee crisis brought the question of immigration to the forefront of minds across Europe. Both politicians and media across the political spectrum immediately treated it as a sudden, unpredictable and overwhelming event. A story was presented of global migration being concentrated on the EU, particularly those arriving via the eastern Mediterranean. Such a story conveniently ignored the much bigger worldwide picture. There are approximately 21.3 million refugees globally, with Europe hosting just six per cent of these in 2015 (UNHCR, 2015). There are also both far more internally displaced people – estimated at more than 40 million – and voluntary internal and international migrants than refugees worldwide (UNHCR, 2016).

Numbers matter, but the way in which they are selected, presented and reacted to influences the kind of conversation we have about immigration. The refugee crisis faced by the EU has been not simply about movement or capacity, but about a political challenge: can progressive forces maintain and protect tolerance in the face of the rise of the far right within the EU's borders? For the UK on the cusp of Brexit, a similar challenge exists: how should those who believe there is a better conversation to be had about immigration react both to Ukip and to their own colleagues within the traditional

parties who themselves have become bogged down in an extremely
negative and divisive discourse on the 'problem' of immigration?

The UK has taken few refugees from the crisis and public debate
has most recently been preoccupied with immigration from elsewhere in the EU, making it seem at first markedly different to
other countries in Europe. Yet it would be a mistake to imagine
that because the composition of newcomers to the UK differs, the
challenges it faces in tackling the thorny issue of immigration are
somehow unique. The reality is that both the refugee crisis and the
vote for Brexit highlight similar trends: as international movement
has come to the forefront of public consciousness, rightwing populists are using their outspoken opposition to immigration to build
support, become realistic contenders for government and force traditional governing parties in a rightwards direction.

In the UK and elsewhere, they have identified an issue which both
connects with voters from across the political spectrum and to which
mainstream parties have been ill-prepared to respond. States still form
the building blocks of the international order and the referendum campaign and the refugee crisis both offered an opportunity to highlight
governments' supposed inability to perform one of the state's most
basic functions: the power to control its own borders. This has proved
particularly potent at a time when disillusioned populations have
experienced extensive political and economic turmoil in recent years.
Already vulnerable due to wage stagnation, job losses and housing
crises, they have been additionally struck by a deterioration in their
sense of security and control. Parties that have responded slowly have
frequently found themselves ejected from office or tumbling in the
polls, while there has been an increasing gravitation towards those
who promise to protect voters in the face of the unknown.

IMMIGRATION AFTER BREXIT

Since the referendum result, the British debate has centred around
what should be done about immigration. Ukip has continued to

pressure the Conservative government for a reduction in absolute numbers and it looks certain that single market access will be sacrificed in order to ensure the end of free movement. Meanwhile, many Labour MPs panicked that their constituents voted leave, have been pressing for the party to demonstrate a harder line on immigration.

The influence of populism has arguably been the main driver of the government's reaction to the referendum, with Theresa May placing immigration at the heart of her Brexit strategy. The political difficulties of Ukip have, if anything, been a consequence not of its policy failure but of its very success in getting its narrative on immigration adopted by the Conservative government and, thus, the need for its existence as a separate entity questioned. The Conservative right has dismissed dissenting voices as attempting to frustrate the 'will of the people' as expressed on 23 June. There has, though, been a vocal backlash from civil society groups, members of the general public and some immigrant communities – though others voted leave precisely to close the door behind them. Many argue that numbers do indeed need to fall and that the country is simply under too much strain from immigration. Others contend that dealing with immigration is in fact primarily a question of challenging perceptions and responding more effectively.

Immigration policy certainly matters. Deciding who can enter a country, through which channels and for how long is a deeply sensitive and complex task for any government. The focus of this book, however, is not on mapping out a detailed plan for how immigration policy will work for the UK post-Brexit. Instead, it is concerned with considering the narratives that have been constructed around immigration and how the conversation might be steered onto a more productive track: one that acknowledges the realities of interconnectedness in a modern, globalised world and addresses the complexity of challenges posed by immigration, rather than seeking to apply blame and sow further division.

The analysis in this book considers progressives as actors who wish to advance the debate about immigration beyond the divisive 'us versus them' thinking championed by rightwing populists, towards a more realistic and productive approach that can produce better outcomes for all of society, established residents and citizens of the UK and immigrant populations alike. There are progressive political actors in all of the mainstream British parties and political parties are a key focus. Their success in reconnecting with the public also requires the formation of alliances with actors outside of the traditional political sphere. What role those actors might play is considered here.

To do this in a time of change and uncertainty, it is prudent to consider what can be learned from how other European countries have responded to the populist challenge on immigration. The focus here is on a comparative approach, understanding how rightwing populism is occurring and being dealt with in other north-west European countries impacted by immigration and on what the UK in particular can learn from that experience. In addition to the UK, three countries are selected for detailed investigation, each of which is currently experiencing a challenge from rightwing populism. The first is France, a key defender of the EU project with a long history of dealing with integration issues and home to arguably one of the most potent far-right parties in Europe, the National Front (FN). The others are Germany and Sweden. Since the refugee crisis and their initial decision to accept significant numbers of refugees, both countries have experienced a striking transformation from their position as the bastions of open and tolerant Europe to states under political strain and with national elections looming in 2017 and 2018 respectively.

CHARTING A NEW PATH

Given the vast wealth of information and theory available on the field of migration, the following analysis attempts to highlight a few particularly pertinent trends and areas for consideration. The time period it explores begins with a broad overview of migration from the mid-20th century and subsequently concentrates in further detail on patterns over the past decade, with particular attention to developments since the beginning of the refugee crisis. The questions of integration, Islam and the management of diversity are considered as key parts of the story of how immigration is discussed and debated today. The data is drawn from a mixture of desk research, interviews with key individuals in the relevant countries and participation in discussion seminars conducted throughout 2016 and in early 2017.

Understanding how to improve the conversation about immigration necessitates a consideration of how narratives have been constructed and developed over time, the strategies anti-immigration populist actors have pursued, and how mainstream parties have reacted. To move forward, we need to understand the past as well as the present and recognise that political choices have consequences: good, bad and sometimes unexpected. Untangling the mix of issues that feed into the public's sense of discontent in European countries reveals that things are not always what they seem and that the question of immigration has always been controversial and far too nuanced to be dealt with by simplistic responses. Mainstream actors ready to take back control must find ways to address this complexity, while maintaining relevance to voters and their experiences. Already, there are many examples of how this can be done effectively and many of the same principles apply regardless of the volume or type of immigration experienced. There is a wide range of possible interventions available to progressives who choose not to despair but to look, listen and learn.

EXISTING NARRATIVES

In the 21st century, individuals, political parties and entire countries are all searching for the answer to the question of who they are and what they stand for. As a globalised economy and challenges that transcend borders have eroded people's sense of self and certainty, populist parties in Europe and elsewhere have gained ground by offering them a way to restore it. Populism thrives on the simplicity of the stories it tells and purports to offer easy solutions to complex problems. Across the UK and Europe, mainstream parties have struggled to keep up, hindered by eroding trust among populations, both voters and non-voters, whom they have disappointed for too long.

The recent success of rightwing populism has had hostility to immigration at its core. Ukip, a once fringe party that failed to secure support for UK 'independence' from the EU on economic grounds, nonetheless helped secure the Brexit vote through, in large part, capitalising on fears about immigration. In France, the anti-immigrant National Front moved from unpopular outlier to serious contender for the presidency in 2017. And in Germany and Sweden, a desperate desire to maintain openness in the face of a great humanitarian crisis has been challenged by the rise of the Alternative für Deutschland (AfD) and the Sweden Democrats respectively.

The story presented by each of these parties is familiar: an unstoppable tidal wave of immigrants is beating down Britain and Europe's doors, facilitated by mainstream politicians and the distant bureaucrats of the EU. The presentation of immigration as a threat creates a powerful 'us versus them' narrative, which plays on the emotions. The style of politics promoted by Ukip and its populist counterparts around Europe is no longer the vague danger of a decade ago, but an imminent threat to mainstream parties. This threat exists on two fronts. First, and most obviously, they risk a continued loss of actual votes and support. Second, in their efforts to remain popular and relevant, they risk being pushed rightwards in their own rhetoric and policies, to a point beyond recognition. This makes getting it right on immigration a matter of survival for mainstream parties. This chapter explores how existing narratives about immigration have been constructed over time and how they have developed since the rise of the new far right and the refugee crisis, in the UK and beyond.

POLITICS AND POLICY ON IMMIGRATION SINCE 1945

Immigration may be front and centre of British and continental European politics today, but this is by no means the first time it has been there, nor is it the first time it has been deeply controversial. Since the end of the second world war, there have been a number of cycles of movement, each accompanied by the creation and development of narratives about immigration and immigrants, opposition to newcomers including from the far right, and mainstream policy reactions and failures.

In the years after the war, the UK found itself facing an acute shortage of labour at the same time as the mammoth task of reconstructing the British economy. The solution adopted was to seek out able-bodied immigrants to assist in the rebuilding effort. These immigrants came primarily from other countries across Europe and from the Commonwealth countries, particularly the Caribbean,

India and Pakistan. Commonwealth immigration was facilitated by the passage of the 1948 British Nationality Act, which offered the opportunity for all Commonwealth citizens to enter Britain freely. Their arrival on Britain's shores was famously symbolised by the docking in Essex of the SS Empire Windrush after a voyage from Jamaica in June of that year. The increasing number of immigrants in the following years led to rising social tensions, centred primarily on concern about competition for jobs and housing against a wider background of poverty. These were stoked and encouraged by nationalist groups like the Union for British Freedom which distributed leaflets urging the public to oppose immigration and operated under slogans such as "Keep Britain White". Beginning in Liverpool in 1948 and continuing through the 1950s, Britain saw race riots which frequently pitted the white working class against recently arrived black immigrants. This culminated in the August 1958 Notting Hill riots, which spread across north-west London and resulted in the arrest of around 140 people, with large fines and lengthy prison terms imposed on some of the participants.

This history and early postwar tension centred on non-European immigrants helps explain the development of race relations legislation in Britain in the 1960s, at the same time as the ongoing civil rights movement was gathering momentum in the United States. The 1965 Race Relations Act outlawed racial discrimination in public places, but failed to address housing and employment and covered discrimination under civil rather than criminal law, leading to strong criticism by some Labour members. Efforts to extend its reach under the subsequent 1968 Race Relations Act prompted the former Conservative cabinet minister Enoch Powell to make his infamous "Rivers of Blood" speech (Bourne, 2015). The speech, delivered to a Conservative association conference in Birmingham, usefully if disturbingly, articulated some of the central ideas that remain at the heart of anti-immigration narratives today: that there are simply too many immigrants and they risk overwhelming Britain's ability to cope; that they are of the wrong kind; and that the English in particular are being "persecuted" by changes to their society on which "they were never consulted". The speech was, of course, devoid of any meaningful reference to the reality of the breadth of challenges faced by immigrants in Britain, or the responsibilities borne by the country following decolonisation, instead calling it a "delusion" to believe that a majority of immigrants were interested in integration, which Powell defined as becoming more or less indistinguishable from the host population (Powell, 1968). Powell's frontline political career ended when he was sacked from the shadow cabinet by Ted Heath, but the battle lines he had drawn – between those seeking to fight discrimination and those fearful of too much and too pressurising a change – lived on and are still evident in today's discussions. Further legislation followed, with victories for both sides. In just two examples, the 1971 Immigration Act placed restrictions on the residency rights of Commonwealth citizens, while the 1976 Race Relations Act created the Commission for Racial Equality (later part of the Equality and Human Rights Commission).

Postwar France and Germany found themselves facing similar tensions as they sought to wrestle with the challenges posed by integrating newcomers and hostility from the domestic population. Both countries experienced immigration from Europe and from further afield. Like the UK, they used immigrant labour, while France also sought to fashion a new relationship with its former colonies. France's European immigrants came from across the continent, while decolonisation led almost 1.5 million French citizens to travel to France from abroad, the vast majority from Algeria. The country also accepted large numbers of refugees from the Vietnam war (Hein, 2004). Both East and West Germany set up 'guest worker' schemes to recruit people to perform largely manual labour. East Germany's new faces came primarily from the eastern bloc, as well as further afield from Cuba and parts of Africa and Asia. The West German scheme was much larger, initially recruiting from European countries and later growing to include Morocco and Tunisia, but it was the expansion of the scheme to include Turkish workers in 1961 that transformed the German immigration experience. Turkish guest workers were welcomed by politicians because they were young and cheap and because it was envisaged that they would stay on temporary visas only while Germany required them. Often illiterate, they were frequently recruited from the poorest areas of Turkey. On arrival, they were housed together in dormitories alongside their compatriots beside the factories in which they worked, thus giving them little chance to learn German. Most expected to return home after a few years. With time, however, the newcomers proved themselves hard workers and German businesses came to rely on them, resulting in mounting and ultimately successful pressure on government to allow extensions of stay. Without any real planning, the settled Turkish population therefore burgeoned, but few of the rights and opportunities they would need to fully integrate and succeed in German society were made available to them. Gradually, Turkish settlers brought their families to join them and moved from dormitories into cheap areas of German cities. In the 1970s, as Germany faced economic challenges, xenophobic rhetoric about non-Germans began to grow and active policies to encourage Turkish workers to return home were pursued, including the provision of financial incentives (Bartsch, Brandt and Steinvorth, 2010).

The Nordic countries meanwhile established a trade agreement in 1952, which created a common labour market and allowed free movement across borders. Immigration to Sweden was subsequently dominated by movements from its Nordic neighbours, primarily Finland, which was used to expand the tax base Sweden needed to develop its welfare state and public sector. The number of refugees arriving and family reunification from Latin America and the Middle East increased from the early 1970s (Westin, 2006). In spite of this, Sweden largely maintained its open, tolerant approach – the Sweden Democrats were founded in 1988, but found little support at that time.

What might be considered a second 'wave' of modern immigration in Europe began in the 1990s, following the end of the cold war and the ensuing conflicts in the Balkans. Much of the political and public debate that surrounded it concentrated at first on refugees, but in the 2000s expanded to much wider discussions: about integration and Islam in the wake of 9/11 and about economic migration following the eastward expansion of the EU. As Yugoslavia collapsed in a bitter civil war, both the UK and France were initially reluctant to take in refugees. The former advised they be assisted closer to their country of origin, while the latter supported the creation of safe havens within conflict zones, a policy pursued by the UN with disastrous humanitarian consequences in such cases as that of Srebrenica in July 1995 (Human Rights Watch, 1995). In political and media discussions, the crisis was widely branded the worst facing Europe since the 1940s. Germany, which accepted some 350,000 refugees from Bosnia in the early 1990s, grew increasingly irate with its fellow Europeans' refusal to share the burden and took steps to limit their stay in the country, which included only granting temporary protection and the signing in 1996 of an agreement to repatriate all refugees from Yugoslavia, following the end of the war in Bosnia (Borkert and Bosswick, 2007).

Under a new Labour administration which came to power in 1997, the UK took larger numbers of refugees from the Kosovo war. By 2002, asylum applications had reached their peak. In that year, applications stood at 84,132 and asylum applicants together with their dependents comprised 44% of net migration (Migration Observatory, 20 July 2016). This was not without a backlash. Although its opponents were no longer concentrating on skin colour, they took on a strikingly similar tone to those who had challenged immigration in the postwar years: presenting refugees as a drain on resources while simultaneously questioning their right to be in the country. Expanding mass media on a scale that had not previously existed, including burgeoning internet coverage in the early 2000s, put increasingly negative information about refugees in the hands of more and more people. A 2000 survey conducted by Ipsos MORI in Britain found 80 per cent of respondents believing refugees came to the country primarily because they considered it a "soft touch" and it was during this period that terms such as "failed" and "bogus" asylum seekers were popularised (Karpf, 2002).

Though immigration to the UK had exceeded emigration at points during the 1980s, it was from 1994 that net migration began its relatively steady rise. In addition to the movement of those fleeing conflict, the freedom of movement rights introduced by the Maastricht treaty had changed the dynamic. Already attracting large numbers of immigrants for the purpose of work, the UK then made the now infamous decision (accompanied only by Sweden and Ireland) not to impose transitional controls on workers from countries joining the EU in 2004. This resulted in the country's first exposure to large-scale immigration of eastern European workers, at a rate vastly underestimated by the then government (Bale, 2014).

During its time in power from 1997–2010, Labour made six major legislative changes as well as a host of amendments to immigration rules.[1] Its approach during this period can be identified as two-pronged: on the one hand, concentrating on a security-based approach to protecting the UK's borders from illegal immigration and, on the other, introducing measures to promote integration. Very little attention was directed to preventing those who wished to come to the UK legally from doing so. While the Conservatives had already abolished exit checks in 1994 for those departing to EU destinations, Labour extended this to all travellers in 1998. Routes for those wanting to work in the country were widened: the highly skilled migrant programme was introduced, followed by a points-based system for non-EU migrants. Labour also abolished the primary purpose rule (thus more easily allowing spouses of British nationals to join them permanently) and in 1999 launched the prime minister's initiative, which was successful in its aim of substantially increasing the number of non-EU students in the UK. David Goodhart (2010) has suggested that the rise in immigration that resulted from such policies was accidental in its scale, while organisations such as Migration Watch (2015) have criticised the then government for failing to publicise its decisions, feeding into the sense among some voters that large-scale immigration occurred without the public's consent, and fostering a sense of distrust on the issue of immigration that continues to plague the Labour party today.

By 2005, the Conservatives were already picking up on frustration among voters and immigration featured heavily in that year's general election campaign. The party's manifesto, Time for Action (2005), called repeatedly for "controlled immigration". The proposals put forth included withdrawing from the 1951 Refugee Convention and "taking back control" of asylum policy "from Brussels". Interestingly, the argument, though mainly about security, was framed in terms of a humane and commonsense approach, while recognising the benefits immigration had brought to the UK. An "overall annual limit" to immigration was promised and the tagline "it's not racist to impose limits on immigration" used to sum up the overall message. Though the Tories lost that election, by 2010, immigration was among the most prominent issues featured in the party's campaign. Again, the Conservative manifesto promised an upper limit on immigration, but this time it went further, specifying it at "tens of thousands" (Conservative Party, 2010). After forming a government, the Conservative-Liberal Democrat coalition did take steps to reduce immigration, though the specific target was never actually included in the coalition agreement (Hampshire and Bale, 2015). The government abolished the post-study work scheme and reduced visa options for workers and family reunion.

But the promise to take immigration back to levels last seen in the 1990s proved to be the Tories' 'transitional controls' moment – deeply damaging trust in the government's ability to get immigration under control. It never made any sense to set an arbitrary target and then dig around for ways to meet it. Immigration policy is typically made the other way around: examining what is needed in the labour market and society and then setting quotas on that basis. Indeed, many businesses have been strong opponents of restrictive immigration policies and their lobbying has acted as a counter to harsher government targets (Hampshire and Bale, 2015). In addition, the government had no control over EU immigration, which continued to rise. By 2014, David Cameron had downgraded the target to an "ambition" (Griffith, 2016) and Ukip topped the poll in the European parliament elections.

In France, the 2000s saw falling net migration, but rising concern over integration, with a long-standing debate about the French republic and religious expression growing thornier. Spurred by incidents such as the 2005 riots, the country spent much of the decade searching for ways to ease tensions. In 2004, it had outlawed the hijab and other religious symbols in schools under the official national policy of 'laïcité' (that is the neutrality of the state towards religious beliefs and the separation of the religious and government spheres). By 2007, a reception and social integration contract had been introduced, which required all newly arrived immigrants with legal status to commit to learning French and becoming familiar with French laws. In 2009, the government launched a controversial "great debate on national identity", which sought to explore, with public involvement, the meaning of being French (Simon, 2012).

As recently as 2008 and 2009, Germany experienced net emigration, compounding its demographic problems with an ageing population. But even as it cast around for ways to attract more immigrants, it continued to face challenges on integration with the historically disadvantaged Turkish community. By 2010, Angela Merkel was declaring that multiculturalism had failed, a sentiment echoed by Cameron in early 2011. Across Europe, the trend in the 2000s was to swing back towards assimilative policies. Sweden, meanwhile, joined the EU in 1995. In spite of its failure to impose transitional controls in 2004, it attracted few workers from eastern Europe; immigration flows from family reunification remained high.

The final, most recent and relevant 'waves' of immigration to consider are those which have taken place since around 2013. After a brief dip below 500,000 in 2012, immigration to the UK continued to climb (Office for National Statistics, May 2016). In 2013, pressure on the EU's external borders from the Syrian civil war really began to be felt. By the end of the year, the Italian navy was implementing Operation Mare Nostrum with the support of the European commission and the external borders fund, in response to the increasing wreckages off the coast of Lampedusa, an Italian Mediterranean island closer to Africa than Europe, which proved a popular arrival point for migrants. After the refusal of EU member states to provide extra funding, it was replaced in late 2014 by Frontex's Operation Triton, which had a clearer focus on border protection rather than search and rescue (Frontex, 2014). In 2014, over 170,000 people arrived in Italy by sea (International Organisation for Migration, 2015) and by the end of that year people were starting to arrive in Greece in large numbers in what would become the crisis of 2015. The most damaging narratives that have accompanied these latest developments are partly an extension of historical trends outlined above and partly the result of a change in strategy by rightwing populist parties in Europe.

THE RISE OF THE FAR RIGHT: DETOXIFICATION AND INCREASED FOCUS ON IMMIGRATION

Immigration and the suspicion and hostility it can engender are not new. What makes the current situation so concerning is the extent of support for anti-immigration far-right parties, the backlash against liberal institutions and policies, and the extent to which mainstream parties are struggling to fight back. Mainstream parties are facing a challenge to their legitimacy, while globalisation has changed the way economics and politics are conducted. After the second world war, Europe was determinedly focused on rebuilding. In the 1990s, the EU project was strengthening and in the early 2000s it was expanding and enjoying unbridled economic prosperity. Today the union has taken a battering financially and politically, and increasingly struggles to connect with its citizens in spite of a growing range of options for communication across distances using new technologies. As both European and national mainstream politicians have been hammered by crisis after crisis, populist actors have seized the opportunity to reshape themselves from fringe parties to serious contenders for government. Even outside of government, they can powerfully influence both the conversation and the policy agenda on immigration.

Ukip, the National Front and the Sweden Democrats have all existed for several decades, but the support they now command is a very recent phenomenon. The British public overwhelmingly rejected the far-right British National party (BNP) and in 2006 Cameron was cavalier in dismissing Ukip as "fruitcakes, loonies and closet racists" during a phone-in on the LBC radio station (Assinder, 2006). Ukip, in contrast, has managed to reach out to people who feel strongly that they are not racist and would never have considered supporting a party like the BNP. Initially slow to attract support, it managed to improve its fortunes in two important ways. Firstly, it detoxified its image and marketed itself as an 'outsider' party, opposed to a detached and corrupt political elite. In a political system dominated by two parties, both of which had appeared to be converging on the centre ground, Ukip found a way of speaking to voters who no longer felt represented. Ford and Goodwin (2014) have identified Ukip supporters as people who are typically strongly Eurosceptic, dissatisfied with British democracy, nervous about immigration and pessimistic about the economy, as well as being dissatisfied with both major parties' performance. Ukip has increasingly spoken to these people in their terms, presenting its proposals as 'commonsense' options and offering a palatable alternative to the traditional mainstream. Secondly, the party developed a much more forceful focus on immigration, readjusting its primary focus on leaving the EU to one that emphasised leaving the EU as the *only* way to gain control over immigration.

The National Front has pursued a similar strategy. Under Jean-Marie Le Pen, the FN was divisive, its leader prosecuted for Holocaust denial and the party largely concerned with tapping the protest vote. Under Marine Le Pen, it has openly pursued a policy of "de-demonisation", casting off accusations of racism and anti-semitism and attempting to demonstrate its commitment through such concrete actions as the expulsion of Le Pen Sr from the party in 2015. While Jacques Chirac was rightly able to accuse the party of representing the betrayal of French republican values when Jean-Marie Le Pen reached the second round of the presidential election

in 2002, the FN has now positioned itself as the only party committed to protecting French identity and restoring national pride. It has
railed against the failures of the EU in recent years and, like Ukip,
exploited the sense of distrust and anger among the general public,
at a time when faith in mainstream parties, and especially the French
Socialist administration, has been extraordinarily poor. Though the
FN has always expressed opposition to immigration, the refugee
crisis and terror attacks in France have provided an opportunity for
it to link the issue to the failings of the EU and capitalise more effectively on people's fears. The party focuses on both legal and illegal
immigration, vowing to reduce net migration to France to 10,000
annually. It also supports ending the Schengen area (which allows
passport-free travel between 26 of the EU's member states), making
it more difficult for immigrants to gain French citizenship and giving priority to French citizens over foreigners in access to jobs and
social housing (National Front, 2017).

The party leading Germany's anti-immigration charge, the Alternative für Deutschland, is both similar and different to its British and
French counterparts. Like Ukip, it has seen off some more extreme
competition in the form of the neo-Nazi National Democratic Party
(NPD). Like the FN, it has cast off a former leader, although in
this case it was for being too moderate. The party's founder, Bernd
Lucke, was replaced by Frauke Petry in early 2015, amidst accusations that he was failing to adapt to the demands of its growing
band of supporters. Unlike the others, the AfD is still a relatively
new party, established only in 2013. Its original goal – the abolition of the euro – proved unpopular and under Petry it moved to
the right, emphasising the protection of Germany, focusing force-
fully on immigration and seizing on the discontent generated by the
refugee crisis and terror attacks in Europe in 2015 and 2016. Under
the strain of the refugee crisis, the traditionally anti-immigration
Sweden Democrats have also been able to expand their appeal to a
much broader range of voters worried about what was once a fringe
issue. Many commentators have pointed out that Sweden's famously
strong welfare state requires a robust social contract and high levels

of trust to function – and that that trust begins to break down under the pressure of high levels of immigration.

Key to the far right's success then has been its ability to adapt its strategy in terms of how it appeals to people who are fed-up with the political establishment. It has reached out to unhappy voters from across the political spectrum, co-opting territory from both the right, through latching onto fears about national identity and Europe, and from the left, by expressing concern for workers and struggling welfare states. Merijn Oudenampsen has argued that it was the Dutch far-right politician Pim Fortuyn who paved the way in the mid-2000s for the European far right's new direction. Rather than focusing on conservative social values, as the far right had traditionally done, Fortuyn, he suggests, claimed to be "defending secular, progressive culture from the threat of immigration" (quoted in Polakow-Suransky, 2016). Other parties followed suit. This has provided a powerful narrative that has succeeded in drawing support away from the mainstream.

ELEMENTS OF THE ANTI-IMMIGRATION NARRATIVE

Rightwing populist parties are not alone in creating, directing and perpetuating particular narratives about immigration. Everyone from media to business, workers, security forces, pollsters and civil society, plays a role and it is in part the multitude of voices involved that makes determining how narratives on immigration are shaped and how they can be changed so challenging. Many efforts to stir up hostility to immigrants are blatant and intentional, but some of the real damage is often sustained more subtly, especially when dangerous habits creep into the mainstream discourse without those picking them up necessarily even noticing. In spite of the complexity, it is possible to identify a number of trends that feed into the wider political and public conversation about immigration that has become so negative. Across countries, and in the treatment of different immigrant groups, these tendencies can be detected. They are not reserved for just EU immigrants in one country or refugees in another, but rather show remarkable similarities across time and place.

The obvious place to start is with language. Immigrants of all backgrounds are portrayed by the far right and increasingly by mainstream actors using highly emotive, deeply derogatory and often inaccurate language, whether it is printed, spoken, or posted online. The difficulty in deciding what to call people on the move is emblematic of this debate. 2015 and 2016 saw a plethora of short articles in the press trying to distinguish between migrants, refugees and asylum seekers. Those who work with people fleeing conflict often claim that designating someone as an 'economic migrant' is a tactic to delegitimise their suffering and draw attention away from their rights under the 1951 Refugee Convention. They also prefer to describe immigrants without formal papers as undocumented or irregular, while government and security forces generally insist on the term 'illegal'.

A common theme across each of the countries examined in this study is the use of 'water words', which are now so ubiquitous in the discourse on migration that they are used by every political group and actor, including many who would overtly describe themselves as 'pro' migrant or refugee, as well as being exceptionally popular across many media platforms. Water words are analogies such as those which talk about flows, streams or waves of immigrants. Water words imply something powerful and pressurising. Anti-immigration forces use them to conjure up threatening images of systems being overpowered and swept away and tend to use the more extreme versions such as 'floods' or the 'tidal wave' referred to at the start of this chapter. In this presentation, there are no individuals with unique stories, only a single, powerful force bearing frighteningly down.

Words do not just communicate, they manipulate, and the far right goes much further. In 2015, the UN high commissioner for human rights, Zeid Ra'ad Al Hussein, condemned a British newspaper columnist's description of migrants as "cockroaches", pointing out its eerie similarity to the language used in Rwanda prior to the 1994 genocide (United Nations, 25 April 2015). In Germany, Petry likened migrants to compost in October 2016 – her argument being that both are colourful. All of this is aimed at dehumanising people who come from a different background, national or ethnic group and feeding a negative, exclusionary sense of national identity among host populations. While some of these comparisons are extreme and have attracted fierce criticism and, in some cases, apologies, they are deeply alarming. So too is the copycat behaviour of mainstream politicians. We should be worried that the far right is increasingly setting the tone for our discussions. As early as 2002, Labour's home secretary, David Blunkett, was referring to the children of asylum seekers "swamping" British schools, and in 2015, Cameron referenced a "swarm" of migrants at Calais.[2] Apparently frightened by the success of the populists, mainstream parties seem to be seeking to emulate them to try and win back lost voters. In doing so, they are failing to come up with and use their own terminology.

Our modern information culture provides the backdrop against which all discussion about immigration takes place. Though knowledge may be power, we face a saturated 24-hour news and social media environment which risks overwhelming its consumers. A tempting refrain when progressives do not get the result they hoped for – as with the EU referendum – is to complain that people did not have enough information. However, it is precisely the volume of information people have access to that can make it difficult to separate fact and fiction. The rise of fake news and the presentation of misleading claims are particularly problematic when people are forced to take shortcuts to deal with this volume of data. They look to people they trust, but evidence suggests that levels of trust in politicians, experts and the mainstream media are especially low among those displaying anti-immigration tendencies. This creates a space for rightwing populists to fill.

Yet the mainstream media also provides a platform for negative rhetoric, which some new media outlets have fed off. This is the latest manifestation of a trend that has existed in the UK for quite some time. While the partisan nature of Britain's printed press is no secret, when analysed it is striking the extent to which print media in particular use certain language. The Migration Observatory at Oxford University (7 November 2016) carried out a study of the print editions of 11 national British newspapers from 2006–15, exploring their coverage of the migration debate while recognising that they play a role in contributing to national policy narratives. It found "mass" to be the most common way of describing immigration in the press during this period. "Illegal" was the most common qualifier associated with "immigrants" or "migrants". Opposition to mass immigration is a hallmark of policy among rightwing populist groups, but there is no agreed widespread definition of what this actually means: how many immigrants constitute 'mass' immigration? Again, it is the focus on pressure rather than detail that matters. Immigration is being presented as something which places unbearable strains on UK, with which it cannot cope.

The impact of the press on public opinion on any political issue is notoriously difficult to measure. However, it is worth exploring a few further trends. The same Migration Observatory study found that from the election of the Conservative-led coalition in 2010, the volume of coverage on immigration rose sharply, especially when measures to reduce net migration were introduced in 2011 and 2012. The focus on EU migrants grew from 2012, particularly after transitional controls on labour market access for Romanians and Bulgarians were removed in 2014. The focus also shifted in 2009 and onwards from the legal status of migrants to a much stronger emphasis on the scale of migration, accompanied by an increasing focus on the relative importance of limiting or controlling migration. In some regards, it seems reasonable to conclude that reporting was simply reflecting changing policy. Yet the study also discovered a tendency for the press to blame politicians for the scale of EU migration. Moreover, this was presented in an overwhelmingly negative light, with 69 per cent of articles on this topic mentioning only problems. More worryingly, it identified an inclination among journalists themselves to frame the migration debate, rather than simply reporting it. In 41 per cent of articles on EU immigration, no additional sources were cited to support assertions made in the story.

How then does Britain's coverage compare to its continental neighbours? A study of five European countries commissioned by UNHCR and carried out by the Cardiff University School of Journalism (2015) set out to study the reaction of print media to growing immigration in 2014 and the refugee crisis in 2015. It found wide variations in how national media reported immigration and asylum news. The British media was among those most likely to concentrate on "threat themes" and was the most negative and polarised, with Sweden's press being the most positive. The study also explored who is given a voice in the migration debate, examining the most commonly cited sources. In all countries, politicians were close to the top and the governing party or coalition tended to dominate political sourcing. But in the UK and Sweden, those voices who were reported opposing government policy were most likely to come from the anti-immigration far right, whereas in Germany they came primarily from the Green and Left parties. Ukip was given ample attention in the British press, attributed by the authors to its importance as an electoral force. The Sweden Democrats gained increased representation after their electoral victory in 2014. The German far right, by contrast, has lacked a political voice in the German press, apparently due in part to its lack of representation in the national parliament. The UK was identified as a country in which NGOs were more prevalent in media, in part because mainstream parties were seen as less willing to make the case for liberal policies on immigration; in Sweden NGOs were less present, but humanitarian themes overall more common.

Since the second world war, politics in the western world has advanced a great deal, or tried to, towards more collaborative approaches. With the end of the cold war, many grew complacent about the triumph of a liberal-democratic ideology. Yet it now appears that an 'us versus them' mentality is back. Such a politics allows people to believe that their side is righteous and correct, enabling well-intentioned people to justify all kinds of actions and behaviour, for example setting aside the law when it comes to the treatment of particular groups. Anti-immigrant forces often apply a 'deserving migrants' narrative to their approach to those they view as outsiders. They can then wrap up dangerous propositions in a harmless-sounding appeal to common sense. According to this thinking, it is possible to say some human beings deserve our empathy, but then conveniently single out and mistreat those who do not.

In Britain, the 'deserving migrants' narrative is most familiar in the form of arguments about welfare tourism. The 2014 British Social Attitudes Survey found 24 per cent of respondents expressing a belief that immigrants came to Britain mainly to live off welfare, rather than to work, study, or claim asylum. The belief was particularly strong among those who disapproved most of immigration. The question of deserving migrants has more recently manifested itself in the leave campaign's complaint that EU immigration was placing too much strain on public services, particularly the NHS. It is also at play in conversations about whether child refugees from Calais should be accepted into the UK, and has been at the heart of a debate over the fiscal contributions economic immigrants make to the public purse.

Probably the most widely cited study finding that immigrants to the UK contribute more than they take out comes from UCL work by Dustmann and Fratini (2013). This found that European Economic Area immigrants made a net fiscal contribution of about £22.1bn between 2001 and 2011, or gave back 34 per cent more than they took out, while non-EEA immigrants made a contribution of £2.9bn, or gave two per cent more than they took out. The 'native' population made an overall negative fiscal contribution of £624.1bn. These findings are backed up by other studies. Yet organisations such as Migration Watch (2014) have countered with their own studies. These begin with different assumptions and conclude by claiming a negative fiscal contribution from immigrant groups. In discussing the deserving nature of immigrants, and trying to objectively prove oneself right by referring to whichever data supports their side, those participating in the immigration debate often end up further cementing distrust and talking past one another, instead of engaging in meaningful dialogue and compromise. Undecided voters can end up even more confused than previously and this can lead to a further hardening of the debate (Katwala et al, 2014).

ISLAM, SECURITY AND INTEGRATION

The deserving migrant narrative is one that has recently been most strikingly applied to Muslims. Recent jihadist attacks on European soil have provided useful 'evidence' for rightwing populists and their growing ranks of supporters that something is intrinsically wrong with Islam and that it is in conflict with the values of their countries. Not only can those of the Muslim faith be presented as a threat, but rightwing populist parties can be presented as virtuous protectors, allowing them to create a complementary narrative around security and protection. This is then used to justify actions many ordinary people would not otherwise consider acceptable. One of the most profound effects of the refugee crisis on the narratives surrounding immigration has been to merge the conversation on Muslims and refugees, usually resulting in the painting of both as one large, undesirable block. For the UK, with its population of roughly three million Muslims, this wider context matters and has the potential to stir up hostilities last activated after the attacks of 9/11 and 7/7.

In France, Renaud Camus' (2011) theory of "grand remplacement" has been eagerly adopted and popularised by the FN. The idea that France is losing its identity demographically, being replaced by a new population of immigrant ethnicity, seems far more plausible in the context of more than one million refugees from primarily Muslim countries of origin entering Europe in 2015. Although France has received comparatively few of these, their presence in Europe is enough to stoke concern. Following the November 2015 Paris attacks, some felt threatened on two fronts. Some of the attackers were born and raised in France, feeding theories about problems with integration, while two of the Stade de France attackers carried

Syrian passports, raising fears that the refugee inflow is being used by terrorists to 'infiltrate' the continent. Germany, long shielded from terrorism, experienced a number of small-scale attacks in 2016. Even before this, at its party conference in May 2016, the AfD adopted a manifesto that declares "Islam is not part of Germany" (Bellon, 2016). Petry has also expressed concern that the achievements of the Reformation and the Enlightenment are in danger and a representative of AfD and MEP declared on Twitter that those murdered at Berlin's Christmas market in December 2016 were "Merkel's dead".

Highly publicised attacks on women are also presented as proof by anti-Muslim forces that Islam is incompatible with European values. In Germany, the 2015 New Year's Eve sex attacks presented a golden opportunity to emphasise this. Around 1,200 women across the country were attacked by men acting in groups, reported by police to be of Arab or North African appearance. Most of the incidents were in Cologne, but attacks were also reported in Hamburg and other cities (Noack, 2016). In Sweden, a number of attacks on young women at music festivals were also reported to be linked to men of immigrant origin. In both cases, there was intense anger at the initial failure of the media to report these incidents, contributing to conspiracy theories about the mainstream media. Disturbingly, the word 'lugenpresse' (lying press) was used to describe the mainstream media in Germany, a phrase historically directed against newspapers critical of the Nazis (the Economist, 6 October 2016).

It is perfectly reasonable to respond to terrorist attacks and attacks on women with concern, new security measures and an investigation into what actually happened. All violence is reprehensible and to do less would be negligent. The populist response, however, tends to be one that paints large groups of diverse people as homogeneous threats. It is also devoid of context, such as acknowledging terrorism by individuals of other faiths or indeed the far right itself, or the role of poverty and class, rather than simply ethnicity, in determining the likelihood of people to commit crime (Saunders, 2016). Of course, there is an irony in the far right's new-found concern for women, given its typically restrictive approach to those same women in terms of what opportunities they should be afforded. Its supposed outrage about both sexual attacks and the supposed oppression of Muslim women seem incongruous with its own ideology.

Mainstream forces have increasingly been taking shortcuts in both thinking and policy as well. The mainstream is once again guilty of copycat behaviour, particularly on the centre right. In the UK, Cameron's January 2016 announcement of a £20m English language fund was framed in terms of countering extremism among Muslims (Prime Minister's Office, 2016). The Prevent anti-radicalisation strategy has been criticised for approaching Muslims as enemies rather than partners. As home secretary, Theresa May was closely involved in this approach. Her successor as home secretary, Amber Rudd, seems poised to continue along a similar path. In France, Nicholas Sarkozy competed for his party's presidential nomination last year on a platform that was at times even further right than Le Pen's. Though he lost, his rhetoric highlights how far along the spectrum some mainstream actors are willing to move. In Germany, the Christian Democratic Union (CDU) has long been pressured by its sister party, the Christian Social Union (CSU), to abandon its welcoming policy towards refugees. Having greatly reduced the number of incoming refugees as a result of the EU-Turkey deal in early 2016, the CDU was nonetheless punished in regional elections. Merkel initially illustrated a more restrained response to the populist challenge than the UK or France, making clear that Germany could not refuse to accept foreigners, especially Muslims, as this would contravene the country's own laws and its obligations under international law (Benner, 2016). Under political pressure, this stance began to crumble and the chancellor has since suggested a burka ban in Germany.

These questions of shared (or not) values and trust all make the field of integration, particularly of Muslims, a major battleground in the debate about immigration. It is not just about who is arriving, but about how we approach those who are already here and the impact that has on wider discussion and policy. In Germany and Sweden, even with a falloff in refugee numbers, the people who have already arrived will require particular policies in the coming years to assist with their integration. Acceptance from the public will be key to social stability. In the UK, even with its comparatively small refugee intake and probable future decrease in EU immigration, the country is already incredibly diverse: it is projected that one-third of its population will be from Black and Ethnic Minority (BAME) backgrounds by 2030 (Lawrence, 2016). There is simply no escaping the challenges that diversity will bring in the future. This makes learning how to successfully manage diverse societies a key priority for European countries that have experienced inward migration.

FAILED NARRATIVES AND FIGHTING BACK

The rise of rightwing populism in Europe has understandably alarmed mainstream parties and caused confusion and panic on both right and left, but, to date, they have failed to respond effectively to this challenge. In the UK, the inadequacies of existing narratives to respond sufficiently to people's concerns about immigration were painfully demonstrated during the EU referendum campaign. Anyone in Europe who had hoped the populist challenge would die down and recede has been sorely disappointed and deeply alarmed by the events of 2016. There has been a lot of speculation about what went wrong over time. Broadly, the centre left has been guilty of either ignoring public anxiety, or treating it as a function of economics, assuming arguments about national economic growth could dampen people's opposition. The centre right has developed a habit of making unrealistic promises, that, when broken, have corroded faith not only in mainstream parties but, damagingly, in the political system itself. Both have aped the rhetoric and, at times, even the policy proposals of the populist right. It is worth reflecting on the fact that Britons voted to leave the EU despite Ukip barely gaining a foothold at Westminster.

The fact that action on immigration has been prioritised by the prime minister in what little is known of her plan for the Brexit negotiations sends a clear signal that it is now being taken seriously.

It is now irrevocably on the mainstream agenda and it will remain there. But as Britain's government crafts a new immigration regime, there are still a multitude of choices to be made. Even with a hard Brexit that ends full freedom of movement, immigration will continue. The vision of a global Britain will depend on effective trade deals and countries such as India have already indicated that better access for their citizens to the UK will be a prerequisite. The reality of trade-offs in order to prosper will not disappear just because the UK is outside the EU. There is no opt-out clause from globalisation. Mimicking populist rhetoric may lead to short-term gains in the polls, but it is an inadequate and potentially dangerous strategy for tackling one of the biggest issues which currently stands at the intersection of domestic politics and foreign relations. To advance towards more constructive dialogue and action on immigration, progressives need to create their own narratives and policy responses. In this respect, Brexit may offer a silver lining – a chance to finally get the UK's conversation about immigration back on a more productive track. If progressives wish to do this, they need to start by taking a step back from the noise and understanding what is actually going on with immigration and how the public truly feels about it.

NOTES

1. The Government introduced the following pieces of legislation between 1997 and 2010: the Immigration and Asylum Act 1999; Nationality, Immigration and Asylum Act 2002; Asylum and Immigration (Treatment of Claimants, etc.) Act 2004; Immigration, Asylum and Nationality Act 2006; UK Borders Act 2007; and the Borders, Citizenship and Immigration Act 2009.

2. Blunkett's comments echoed earlier sentiments by Margaret Thatcher: http://www.margaretthatcher.org/document/103485, and were referenced by Michael Fallon in 2014: http://www.telegraph.co.uk/news/uknews/immigration/11191766/David-Blunkett-Michael-Fallon-was-right-Britain-is-swamped.html. David Cameron made his comment to ITV news: https://www.theguardian.com/uk-news/2015/jul/30/calais-migrants-make-further-attempts-to-cross-channel-into-britain.

ATTITUDES AND CONCERNS
ABOUT IMMIGRATION

As of 2015, there were 244 million international migrants world-wide according to the United Nations Population Division. These were defined as people living in a country other than that in which they were born and around 76 million of them were in Europe. In 2014, long before the refugee crisis and Brexit began to dominate the headlines, global Gallup polling was finding Europe to be the region of the world with the most negative attitude to immigration – 52 per cent of residents said immigration levels in their countries should be decreased (Esipova et al, 2015). In 2015, EU member states registered over 1.2 million first-time asylum claims according to Eurostat figures. By 2017, Turkey had become home to approxi-mately three million refugees (European commission, 2017).

In some cases, these new developments have brought long-stand-ing public concerns to the fore, while in others they have created new anxieties. Rightwing populist parties that have directed their attention to immigration issues have been so successful because they have tapped into those concerns, which large numbers of voters did not feel mainstream parties had been addressing. They have also made immigration a lightning rod for a whole host of establishment failures. Given the surge in support for the far right, as well as their entry into government in a number of countries, it is tempting to take what it says about public opinion as given. After all, why would people support the far right if they do not agree with what it is saying? However, while populist parties have correctly identified that mainstream parties have been failing on this issue and offered something different, their narrative and agenda is not the only alternative to the status quo that might find support among the public.

Immigration is a complex subject and the conversation around it is fraught with challenges: everything from the manner in which statistics are compiled to the emotional engagement of people at all points on the political spectrum. Mainstream political forces that believe there is a better conversation to be had about immigration must gain a more granular understanding of public opinion. They need to do this in order to ensure that when they craft their responses, they are based on the actual needs and desires of voters, rather than directing their attention only to what the populists want them to focus on and risking exacerbating divisions. Mainstream political actors who believe in democracy have a responsibility both to respond to legitimate concerns and to offer more and better options to those who do not feel listened to and to show them that they can be trusted. Delving more deeply into what is driving concerns about immigration is the first step to addressing them.

This chapter provides an overview of immigration trends and attitudes in the UK, France, Germany and Sweden, in order to better understand where public feeling on immigration currently stands. It draws on a range of data from both before and since the refugee crisis. In particular, it seeks to break down the nature of public anxiety about immigration by exploring attitudes to specific types of immigrants, socio-demographic factors, identity and perceptions of government competence.

WHO'S ON THE MOVE? OLD AND NEW PATTERNS

Figure 2.1 shows overall immigration to the four focus countries, while Figure 2.2 compares annual net migration since 2006.

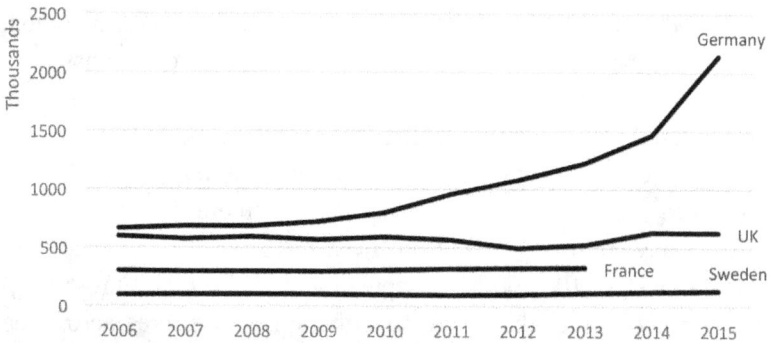

Figure 2.1 Overall Immigration. *Source*: Office for National Statistics, Statistisches Bundesamt, Wiesbaden, INSEE, Statistics Sweden.

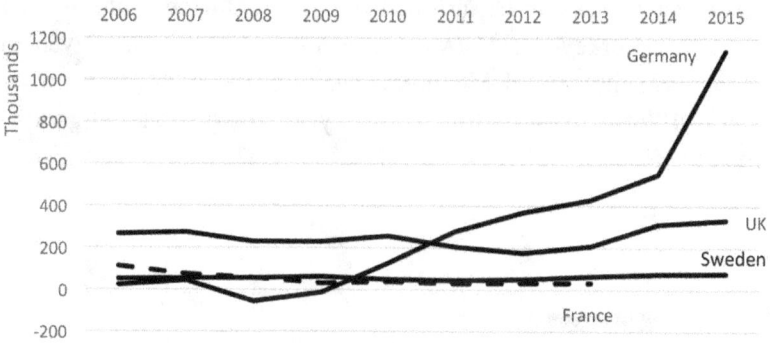

Figure 2.2 Net Migration. *Source*: Office for National Statistics, Statistisches Bundesamt, Wiesbaden, INSEE, Statistics Sweden.

Immigration to all the countries studied has risen during this period, with France the only country to experience a decrease in net migration, caused largely by growing emigration.

The UK and France have experienced comparatively little impact from the refugee crisis, while immigration to Germany and Sweden has been transformed by it. According to the Office for National Statistics, the main reason people immigrate to the UK overall is to work. This also holds true for EU nationals as an independent category; however, the leading reason non-EU nationals come to the country is to study. The numbers of EU and non-EU immigrants to the UK were converging by mid-2016 (Full Fact, 2016). Of the countries focused on, the UK has the most significant share of EU immigrants in its overall mix (European commission, 2015).

As recently as 2009, Germany was a country of net emigration. Arrivals to both Germany and Sweden in 2015 were dominated by asylum seekers from Syria. Germany registered the most first-time asylum applications in the EU that year, while Sweden accepted the most per capita, documenting record immigration. National level figures for 2015 put the number of claims at more than one million in Germany and over 160,000 in Sweden. Figure 2.3 shows asylum applications per 100,000 local population, based on the Eurostat figures, demonstrating the uneven distribution of pressures across the countries examined and compares them to the EU average.

2016 saw a large drop-off in figures in Germany and Sweden, accounted for by the closure of the western Balkan route as well as the EU-Turkey deal. However, over 181,000 people arrived to Europe via the central Mediterranean route in 2016, an approximately 18% increase on the previous year (International Organisation for Migration, 2017).

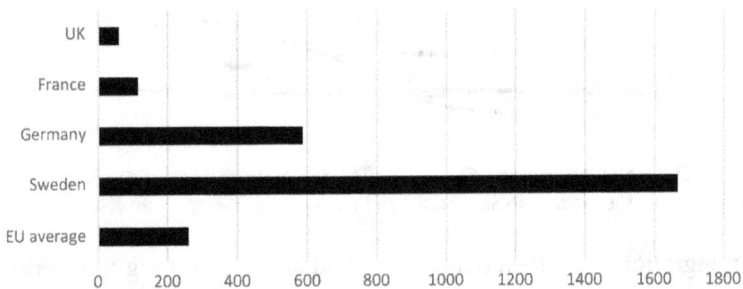

Figure 2.3   Asylum applications per 100,000 local population in 2015. *Source*: Eurostat.

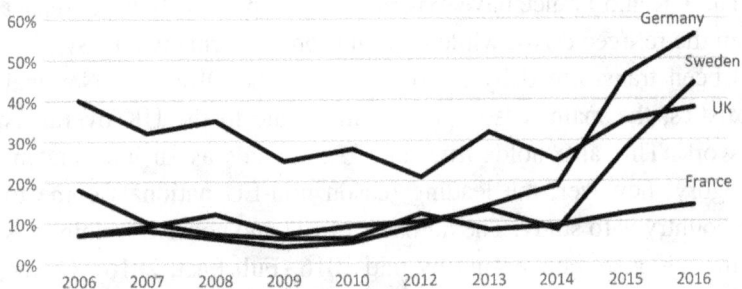

Figure 2.4   Those identifying immigration as a top issue facing their country. *Source*: Eurobarometer, European Commission.

GENERAL ATTITUDES TO IMMIGRATION

In September 2015, Ipsos MORI documented that a record 56 per cent of the British public were mentioning immigration as a concern in its regular Issues Facing Britain Index. A week before the UK's EU referendum, immigration was the number one issue of concern for voters according to Ipsos MORI polling. Afterwards, great effort was expended around the country to discover how big a role it had actually played when people cast their ballots. Since then, there has been widespread agreement that immigration matters to people, but fierce and continuing debate about why. Eurobarometer, the European commission's flagship public opinion poll, regularly surveys EU citizens on their attitudes towards a range of issues. Their feelings on the topic of immigration are quite different depending on whether they are considering it as an issue facing their country (Figure 2.4), an issue facing the EU (Figure 2.5), or something that affects them personally (Figure 2.6).

Considering immigration as an issue for the country, the UK displays relatively high levels of concern over time and France very low levels. Since the refugee crisis began, concern in both countries has increased somewhat, but that in France remains much lower. In Germany and Sweden, the proportion identifying immigration as an important issue is low over time, before showing a significant spike in 2015 and 2016 correlating with the timing of the refugee crisis. Unsurprisingly, all countries show high levels of concern in

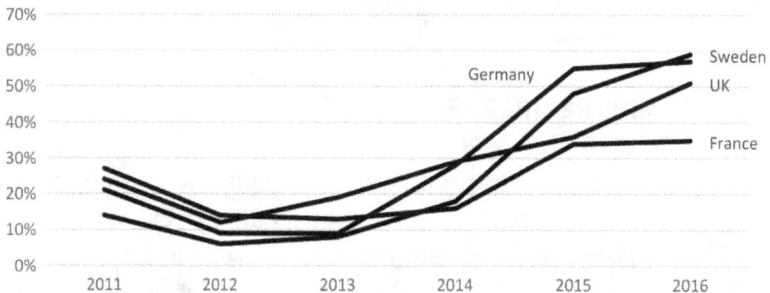

Figure 2.5 Those identifying immigration as a top issue facing the EU. *Source*: Eurobarometer, European Commission.

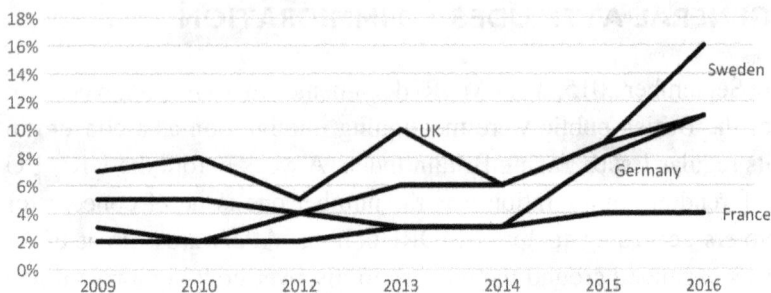

Figure 2.6   Those identifying immigration as an issue affecting them personally.
Source: Eurobarometer, European Commision.

identifying immigration as a top issue for the EU during this time. According to the Eurobarometer survey in autumn 2016, immigration was identified as the top concern for the EU by every member state except for Spain and Portugal.

What is interesting is to compare all of this to whether people feel immigration is affecting them personally. In all countries and over time, the proportion of people reporting that it does is much lower. In addition, many of the areas that voted decisively to leave the EU had little direct experience with immigration in recent years, while cities like London and Manchester, with large overall intakes, voted remain. Surprisingly, in Germany and Sweden, even since the refugee crisis, the proportion of those saying immigration affects them personally is still quite low, at just 11 per cent and 16 per cent respectively in 2016. All of this suggests that across countries, concern about immigration occurs at different levels and is about much more than just numbers.

WHAT ARE PEOPLE WORRIED ABOUT?

With regard to its impact on the host population, anxiety about immigration seems to stem from three main sources. First, there is the worry about the pressure immigration puts on the country's public services and labour market, resulting in fears among the domestic population about the deterioration of both. Second, there is the fear of a negative cultural impact, where immigrants are viewed as a different group who may practice unwanted behaviours, fail to integrate and threaten social cohesion and even national identity. Finally, there is concern about security, the worry that immigrants might actually pose a physical threat, for example through acts of terrorism or crime. All of these fears are present across the four focus countries.

Figure 2.7 shows the level of concern about the impact of immigration on public services. Despite a fall since 2011, this concern remains high in the UK. This is confirmed by 2016's British Social Attitudes Survey (BSA), which recorded 71 per cent of respondents as saying immigration increases pressures on schools across Britain and 63 per cent of people believing immigration increased pressure on the NHS throughout the country. BSA adds another degree of complexity to the levels of concern, by asking the same respondents about their feelings about its impact specifically on their local area. 62 per cent agreed with the statement that immigration increases pressure on local schools, while 57 per cent said it increased pressure on local NHS services. These findings occurred even after respondents had been asked to take into account immigrants' contributions as workers and taxpayers. This feeling of pressure correlates with the leave campaign's message during the EU referendum campaign about a shortage of healthcare services, school places and social housing. This may help explain worries about immigration in areas that have experienced a rapid pace of change,

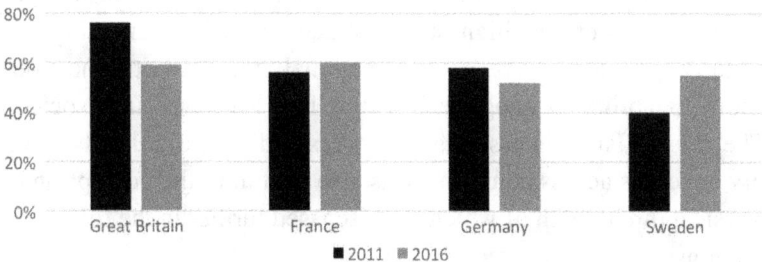

Figure 2.7 Those who think immigration has placed too much pressure on public services in their country. Source: Ipsos MORI Global Advisor Poll 2016.

and where residents thus fear the consequences of diminishing resources. Experience at a local level could also help explain why those living in parts of the UK with poor economic prospects – for example, in deindustrialised regions – often show greater concern about immigration (Ford and Goodwin, 2014) and why they might reject what appears to be strong evidence (referred to in the first chapter) about the overall contribution made by immigrants. Arguments about the economic gains the country experiences as a whole may feel irrelevant and disconnected from their own experience.

In France, despite falling net migration, there has been a slight rise in concern about the impact of immigration on public services and national polling reveals widespread fears the country does not have the resources to cope (IFOP, March 2016). The biggest rise in concern has occurred in Sweden, probably reflecting the fact that its intake of refugees was so large per capita. Surprisingly, concern in Germany, according to Ipsos MORI, has dropped since 2011. While poll data varies, it is striking that in this extracted sample, the UK and France, which have arguably faced much lesser recent pressures than Germany and Sweden, nonetheless show higher overall levels of concern. This suggests that while it is important to take into account measurable pressures, wider political, social and cultural factors also seem likely to influence public feelings about immigration.

Figure 2.8 shows public concern about changes to one's country being caused by immigration. This can be considered one way of measuring how anxious people are about its impact on social cohesion and identity. These worries exceed 40 per cent in every country. Concern is highest in France, probably reflecting the country's debate on the issue of national identity, with questions about its ability to integrate Muslims into a very secular society. The role of Islam is essential to understanding more deeply identity concerns across countries. It is also central to the perception of physical threat, both of which are discussed further in the following sections.

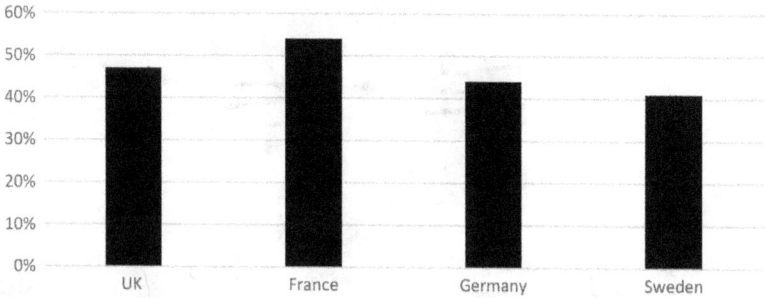

Figure 2.8   Immigration is causing my country to change in ways that I don't like (2016). *Source:* Ipsos MORI.

ATTITUDES TOWARDS PARTICULAR GROUPS

When rightwing populist parties stoke concern about immigration, they often single out particular groups of immigrants, or those of immigrant origin, attempting to strengthen the association between those specific groups and one or more of the threats outlined above. EU immigrants, refugees and Muslims are the three groups which have been the focus of considerable debate in one or more of the countries explored in this study. So how does the public really feel about these groups?

Figures 2.9 and 2.10 show the level of negative feeling by voters towards EU and non-EU immigrants respectively in recent years. Although EU immigration featured strongly in the UK's referendum debate, animosity towards non-EU immigrants has actually been consistently higher for the past three years. The leave campaign saw an opportunity given the growing numbers of, and media coverage about, EU immigrants, referred to in the first chapter, and therefore directed much of their attention to this issue. Both populist and mainstream politicians opportunistically linked specific concerns (pressure on services and the labour market) to EU migration.

The other three countries examined here are similar in that immigrants from outside the EU also elicit more negative feelings than EU immigrants. But they are different in that free movement does not feature much in the public debate. There are specific concerns

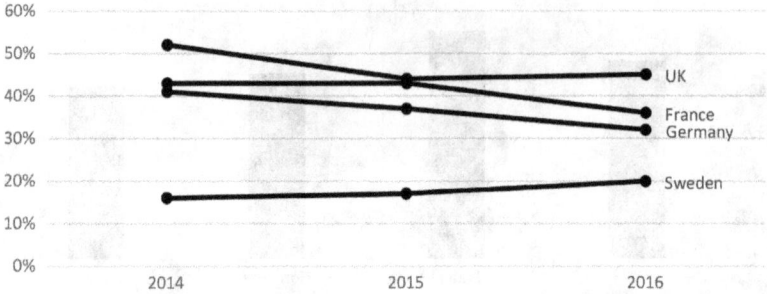

Figure 2.9   Negative feeling towards immigration of people from the EU.
Source: Eurobarometer, European Commission.

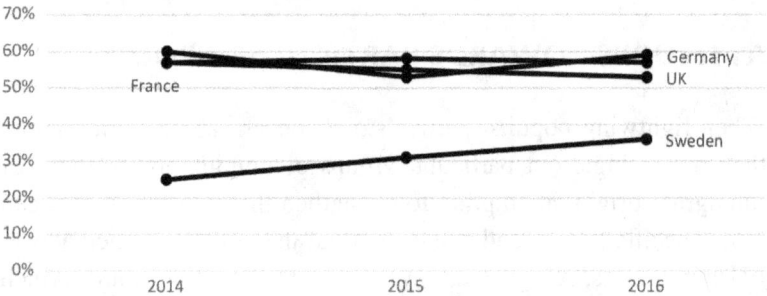

Figure 2.10   Negative feeling towards immigration of people from outside the EU. *Source*: Eurobarometer, European Commission.

in France about fears of "social dumping" caused by EU posted workers (Eurofound, 19 May 2016).[1] Yet in Germany and Sweden, it is largely a non-issue. Far more important are preoccupations with refugees and Muslims. Nonetheless, similarly divisive narratives, which often present immigrants as a threat, exist.

Figure 2.11 illustrates the main concerns associated with refugees by the public in France, Sweden, Germany and Britain in 2016. In three out of four countries, the biggest fear associated with refugees is that they will increase the likelihood of terrorism. In France, where this concern comes second to concerns over jobs and social benefits, it is still high at 46 per cent. Sweden displays a very significant fear about refugees causing crime, also at 46 per cent. Overall, the fear that refugees represent a threat to the public's physical security is high across all countries. This is likely closely linked to attitudes towards Muslims.

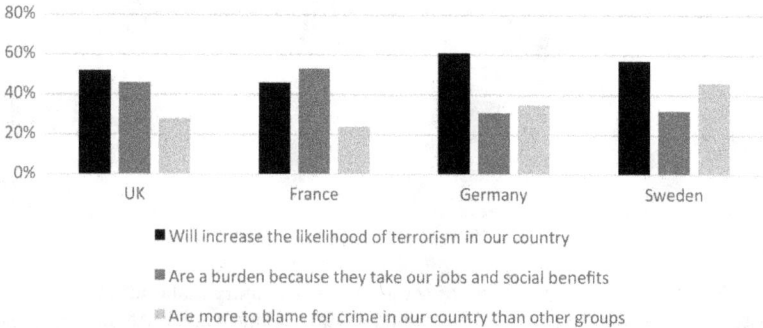

Figure 2.11 Fears about refugees (2016). *Source*: PEW Research Centre, Spring Global Attitudes Survey 2016 (Pew Research Center bears no responsibility for the interpretations presented or conclusions reached based on analysis of the data.)

ATTITUDES AND ISLAM

Unlike the recent surge of interest in refugees, anxiety over Islam and Muslims is more long-established in the focus countries and in Europe more widely. Figure 2.12 compares attitudes to Muslims in 2006 and 2016 – respondents were asked if they had favourable or unfavourable views of Muslims in their country.

While unfavourable views of Muslims have risen in the UK, they dropped in France and significantly in Germany during this time period. In all countries but Sweden, less than one third of the public held a negative view of Muslims in 2016. This suggests progress and a possible growth in public maturity on the topic of Islam following the backlash which occurred after 9/11 and various attacks in Europe in the 2000s. However, figure 2.13 illustrates the extent to which the public believe that Muslims want to form a distinct group rather than adopt the customs of wider society. This is more concerning, with at least 50 per cent in each country still holding this view in 2016.

This perception of difference may explain why concerns and the public discourse about Muslims today tend to focus around the questions of social cohesion, identity and integration. In public perception, with so many arriving from Islamic countries, the term refugee has come to equal Muslim. With the perception of difference between Muslims and non-Muslims, this has contributed to the sense of fear that refugees will carry out attacks against host populations,

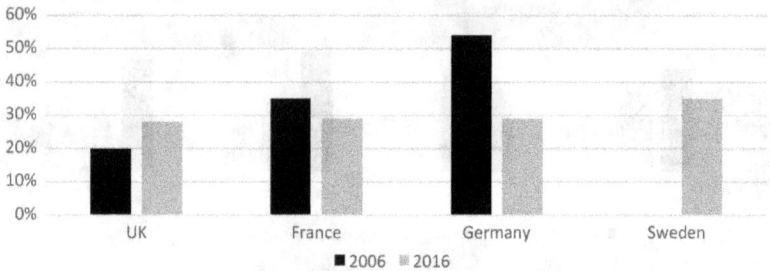

Figure 2.12   Unfavourable view of Muslims in our country (data not available for Sweden in 2006). *Source*: PEW Research Centre, Spring Global Attitudes Survey 2016 (Pew Research Center bears no responsibility for the interpretations presented or conclusions reached based on analysis of the data.)

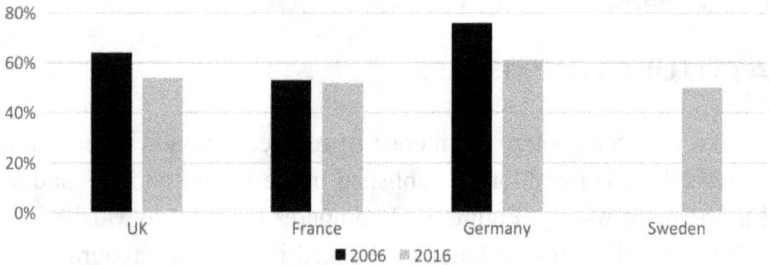

Figure 2.13   Muslims want to form a distinct group (rather than adopt the customs of wider society) (data not available for Sweden in 2006). *Source*: PEW Research Centre, Spring Global Attitudes Survey 2016 (Pew Research Center bears no responsibility for the interpretations presented or conclusions reached based on analysis of the data.)

whose values they are not perceived to share. While the UK continues to receive very small numbers of refugees, the wider European context has also served to stir up hostility towards Muslims in Britain. Following the release of the government-commissioned review by Louise Casey into opportunity and integration in 2016, the questions of identity and Islam are very much on the agenda; they are also likely to attract a renewed focus if, post-Brexit, more attention is directed towards non-EU immigrants.

The perception of Islam as a threat is neither completely new nor wholly irrational, given the history of Europe and its neighbours. For centuries, Christians and Muslims have fought each other for supremacy and this antagonism forms a key part of the history of the continent, with both sides harbouring painful memories. Europeans worried about 'Islamisation' might recall the invasions in the 8th century, followed by centuries of battle to take back control of the Iberian peninsula. Muslim populations who feel marginalised and mistreated in Europe may evoke the memory of the painful colonisation of their countries and the resulting cultural impositions.

Since the 1950s, however, the Muslim population in many European countries has grown through family reunification and high fertility rates into a significant domestic minority (Benton and Nielson, 2013). It is this phenomenon that *is* new, and provides the starting point for more recent unease. In 2010, Muslims formed six per cent of the European population, with 13 million Muslims living in the EU. Worldwide, Islam is the fastest growing religion, expected to overtake Christianity by the end of this century (Hackett, 19 July 2016). Many of those who came 'temporarily', following independence or as guest workers, have stayed. They have also had families, creating a large new community of Muslims who are not immigrants, but who have been born and raised in Europe. Their numbers and visibility have increased greatly, presenting a new experience for many non-Muslim Europeans. For Germany and Sweden, the refugee crisis accelerated the change, bringing large numbers of Muslims not only into the countries, but into communities which may previously have had little contact with them.

In the UK's referendum campaign, the portrayal by the leave campaign of Turkey's potential future membership of the EU as a threat was in part predicated on the fact that it has a Muslim-majority population. While still a cardinal, the previous pope, Benedict XVI, was outspoken in his view of Europe as a cultural continent rather than a geographic one; according to this view Christianity is a key element of Europe and Turkey is not considered a part of it (Gibson, 2011). Criticism is also sometimes levelled at the fact that while Muslims are largely allowed to freely practice their religion in Europe, Christians in Muslim-majority countries continue to be persecuted. Indeed, in countries such as Saudi Arabia, conversion to Christianity is considered apostasy and is punishable by death (Lyons and Blight, 2015).

Much-publicised polling in the UK and France has recently brought these difficult topics once more to the fore. A Channel 4 survey, What British Muslims Really Think (2016), touched on the always-sensitive topic of the treatment of women, with two in five respondents stating that women should always obey their husbands. Over half believed homosexuality should be illegal, and one-quarter supported the introduction of sharia law in parts of the UK. The Paris-based Institut Montaigne (2016) meanwhile carried out a survey which classified its Muslim respondents into six types, with around 28 per cent of the total forming a group considered problematic in the sense of having values opposed to those of the French republic.

Although these figures seem alarming on first reading, a closer examination of both surveys reveals a more mixed picture. The British survey has been critiqued for failing to publicise the results from its control group, drawn from people of other or no faiths. For example, although only 34 per cent of Muslims would report to the police someone suspected of involvement with people supporting terrorism in Syria, the control group figure was even lower at 30 per cent. Its methodology has also been criticised, with polling taking place only in areas with more than 20 per cent Muslim population, which tend to be more economically disadvantaged and socially conservative (Versi, 2016). Meanwhile, the French study found that 46 per cent of Muslims were considered fully secularised, having adopted the French values system, yet this figure was largely lost in the negative coverage of the results.

Such generalisations and an over-emphasis on negative statistics are reflective of a wider trend in which Muslims are too often treated by politicians and the media as a homogenous group. This approach has tended to focus on the group rights debate, looking at the apparently different values of Muslims and non-Muslims in this regard, and concentrating on such issues as the place of women and children and the relationship between religious and political authority (Cherti and McNeil, 2012). This approach is now too often being applied uncritically to refugees as well.

WHO IS DOING THE WORRYING?

There has been a great effort to determine whether supporters of rightwing populist parties share similar characteristics. The most widely documented and well-known theory is that people who support Brexit, Trump and the far right in Europe, and generally dislike immigration, are those 'left behind' by globalisation. Such individuals are more likely to be white, male, older, less educated and less well-off financially. This not only makes sense intuitively, but a wide range of analysis of voting patterns and polling illustrates this trend. Who wouldn't be resentful if prosperity and politics both passed them by? The picture is, however, more mixed than has at times been suggested. If analysts rush to group all those worried about immigration together, they risk copying the populists not only in rhetoric, but in thought process: the idea that political actors can take entire groups of people and successfully orient their response and policy around their supposed group identity without any nuance. On closer examination, just like the variety of concerns about immigration, there is a variety of factors driving it.

On age, millennials are generally more likely to be positive towards immigrants and refugees. Generation X, however, is often worried about its own future and holds more negative views. The National Front is increasingly picking up support from younger voters, with an Odoxa poll at the end of 2016 identifying it as the political party with the most support among those aged 18–34 (Chadwick, 2016). This could reflect support for the party's focus on jobs – youth unemployment stood at 24.2 per cent in the first quarter of 2016 (INSEE), or perhaps a longing for a return to a better past many in this age group don't actually remember. A Tent Foundation survey (2016) exploring attitudes to refugees in Germany found that 35–54-year-olds were the most likely to hold negative positions towards them. More broadly, as populist parties cast off their image as fringe parties with unacceptable views, they are increasingly palatable to younger supporters, who may not be as familiar or turned off by their past associations with racist behaviour as their parents.

Some commentators suggest that AfD supporters are more likely to be young or middle aged, rather than older, with the latter still being largely faithful to the Christian Democrats (Horn, 2016). In terms of voters' economic background, the left behind thesis does not account for middle-class supporters of Brexit or opponents of immigration, nor for differences within working-class opinion.

Some analysts contend that it is really identity and ideology that determines people's views on these issues. Eric Kaufmann's analysis (2016) argues that the strongest predictor of opposition to immigration and support for far-right parties is actually the holding of "authoritarian" values, with a preference for a more stable and orderly world. Moral psychologist Jonathan Haidt's extensive work into how morality is constructed considers how different political beliefs are formed depending on what we value (Haidt, 2012). In exploring nationalism, he finds that many of those opposed to immigration have a real moral commitment to nationalism, and believe in the related social contract in which their government should prioritise the interests of its citizens over those in other countries. This, he argues, is not necessarily racist. "Having a shared sense of identity, norms, and history generally promotes trust", he argues, and higher levels of trust promote a range of benefits for society (Haidt, 2016). There is other evidence from the public that identity matters, too. In the UK, regardless of actual income, those who identify themselves as working class are more likely to be concerned about immigration according to the 2016 British Social Attitudes survey.

Supporters of rightwing populist parties in each country display higher levels of concern about immigration than the general public and, in the UK, political allegiance is now the best indicator of concern on this topic (Ipsos MORI, 2015). However, the general public is also often unhappy with how their government manages immigration specifically. Figure 2.14 shows the level of dissatisfaction with government action on immigration over a five year period prior to the refugee crisis. The Transatlantic Trends survey found that, compared with the same respondents' assessment of overall government performance, dissatisfaction on the specific issue of immigration was much higher, even before the refugee crisis. The UK and France display the most consistently high levels of dissatisfaction on this topic, while Germany and Sweden fluctuate, both surpassing 50% at different points for the period shown (data not available for Sweden before 2013).

Since the onset of the refugee crisis, a wide range of national polling has attempted to measure the evolution of attitudes to government management of immigration. In the UK, dissatisfaction with government in this area has remained high (see, for example, Ipsos MORI, Shifting Ground, 2016), but has not seen very notable change. In France, there has been similarly little overall change, though some polls report that voters do worry that the country does not have the resources to cope with arriving refugees (IFOP, March 2016). In Germany and Sweden, the public has been increasingly frustrated by the pressures placed on their countries. Merkel still enjoys high satisfaction ratings and it is a very realistic prospect that she will win the federal election later in 2017, but her approval ratings remain far below those she previously enjoyed. The worry about government management of immigration is closely associated with a broader fear exacerbated by globalisation and evident across the focus countries: people feel that governments are not in control. In a world still dominated by states, this is an understandably frightening prospect for many. It has been further aggravated

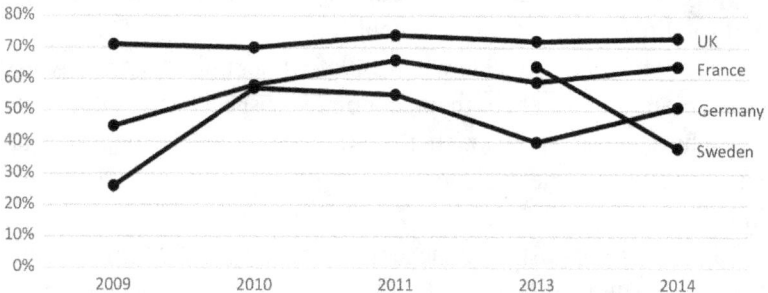

Figure 2.14 Those who think the government is doing a poor job of managing immigration. *Source*: The German Marshall Fund of the United States (GMF) Transatlantic Trends Study.

by the imagery of the refugee crisis and the terrorist attacks of 2015 and 2016. Highlighting and emphasising government failure in the area of safety and security is a favourite tactic of rightwing populists across the focus countries and beyond.

WHERE DOES THIS LEAVE US?

Like the composition of immigration itself, the picture of public attitudes across Europe is mixed and influenced by many factors. It also seems at times contradictory. On the one hand, people report few personal effects from immigration, but on the other show concern about it at a local, national and EU level. In the UK, regions with large numbers of immigrants sometimes welcome them, but animosity towards immigration appears both in communities that have experienced rapid change and those which have seen little immigration. The same concerns are present across all the focus countries, yet they do not always occur in proportions that would intuitively make sense given a consideration of the statistical data on national migratory flows. All of this hints at a diversity of experience and opinions that are nowhere near as simple as the picture painted by populist parties.

The complexity of opinion probably reflects the conflicted nature of the feelings individuals have towards immigration. They may happily live, work and study alongside those from other countries and, at times, recognise their contribution. Yet their fears about immigration are connected to a sense of vulnerability, as they worry much more broadly about their economic prospects, cultural identity and physical safety. Though there are some socioeconomic patterns, there is no one exclusive type of person who is worried about immigration.

Rightwing populists gain success when they exploit pre-existing fears or create new ones, finding ways to exacerbate people's feelings of vulnerability and linking them to pressure from immigration. The uncertainty of globalisation, economic challenges and terrorist attacks make this easier and anti-establishment groups, by their nature, do not have the disadvantage of past records of failure in office, allowing them to more easily attack mainstream parties. Across countries, one of the most worrying trends is the levels of dissatisfaction the public has with the government's ability to manage immigration. When their governments do not appear able to protect them, people go looking for those who claim they will.

Yet their success is not inevitable. Different political and practical decisions by mainstream parties can lead to different outcomes. Progressives need to take back control of the conversation, back their words up with action and challenge the portrayal of the domestic population as the protagonists and immigrants as antagonists locked in an eternal struggle which one group has to eventually win. This will require some difficult admissions and actions. Mainstream parties tempted to copy populists need to understand that this may produce short-term gains, but it is an unsustainable strategy in the long run. Ultimately, it will only leave the public angrier and more disillusioned when their promises fail to deliver. Progressives determined to defend a set of globalist values need to ask whether it is practical or helpful to try and unite people around only one set of specific values, and they should consider whether some of their actions are indeed counter-productive. Many people support populist parties not because they are inherently racist, but because they feel that, given their concerns, they currently have no other choice. It is the responsibility of a well-functioning democracy to respond to this challenge. In order to speak to voters more powerfully than their populist rivals, mainstream forces should recognise both warning signs and positive opinions and work to reconcile them. In spite of the challenges and divisions exposed by the Brexit vote, there is now an opportunity to take a more holistic approach to immigration. This must include addressing the desire for a sense of control, as well as developing an inclusive approach that makes people feel listened to, while ensuring opportunities and support are available for both existing residents and new arrivals to the UK. The second half of this publication now turns to considering how this can be done.

NOTES

1. A posted worker is an employee who is sent by his or her employer to carry out a service in another EU Member State on a temporary basis. The EU regulates this group under the Posted Workers' Directive 96/71/EC.

CASE STUDIES

France, Germany and Sweden are countries that have faced challenges on immigration and integration for years. Though each has a unique political history, all now face a similar threat: anti-immigration, rightwing populist parties are snapping at the heels of mainstream ones and are growing in popularity. In France, the National Front is agitating loudly for a referendum on EU membership, a project that, if successful and if the country voted to leave, could spell the end of the bloc. Germany and Sweden, at the forefront of the refugee crisis, have been forced to adapt under a pressure neither country had seen before, with little real help from their European neighbours and much active opposition. Some admire France for its steadfast approach to promoting a unifying vision of French identity largely based on secularism; others argue that it has backfired, isolating segments of the population and even contributing to an environment that has driven some youths to leave to fight for Isis in Syria and Iraq. Modern Germany and Sweden have long counted openness and tolerance as key tenets of their national identity, but have recently faced a clear and understandable conflict between their desire to uphold these values in the face of adversity and difficult political realities.

Each country has tried to respond to the populist challenge and animosity towards immigration, while in many ways coming under more strain than the UK has ever experienced. The examples outlined in this chapter explore the reaction of governments, politicians, civil society and other actors in France, Germany and Sweden both over time and as a result of the refugee crisis. The examples are grouped into thematic areas, each of which seeks to challenge negative perceptions and messaging on immigration through responding pragmatically to some of the concerns identified in Chapter 2. The benefits, costs and challenges involved in each one are considered in turn. The principal lesson is that dealing with immigration is an ongoing challenge, one requiring constant experimentation, which no country has yet perfected. In dealing with it and responding to the populist challenge, mainstream political actors in these countries have been expanding their spheres of reference, seeking to include and learn from a whole range of new and increasingly important societal actors. They have also pursued innovations that not only seek to respond to the challenges of immigration, but to those of integration, democratic participation, social cohesion and opportunity.

TAKING CONTROL: GOVERNMENT ACTION AND LEGISLATION

One of the great desires of people who are worried about immigration is to see their governments take back control of what is happening in this area. Part of this clearly involves the development of immigration policy itself and deciding who will and will not be permitted to enter the country and on what terms. Yet there are limitations to how much numbers can simply be cut in a globalised world, as well as how much impact this will have on people's sense of control when their fears are complex, as outlined in the previous chapter. In addition, reductions in immigration may run counter to other national goals such as continued economic growth. Net migration targets are also problematic given that a democratic government has no control over emigration, which affects these figures.

There are other ways to establish a sense of control, through better managing those who do come into the country. Previous research has found that "the best test of a legitimate anxiety is whether somebody is interested in a constructive solution to address it" (Stockham, 2014). Those who are genuinely prejudiced will take little interest in such innovation and fight against it, arguing that dramatic reductions or a complete halt to immigration is the only acceptable way forward. But, for the people who are genuinely anxious and seeking reassurance, effective government action and legislation that addresses the challenges thrown up by dealing with newcomers can be useful. The refugee crisis led to a flurry of legislative changes and innovations in Germany and Sweden in order to put in place the infrastructure needed to cope with the unprecedented numbers of people arriving, showing that it is possible to innovate effectively under pressure.

GERMANY: ACTION ON INTEGRATION

The Integration Act was first proposed in Germany in April 2016 and subsequently came into force in August of that year. It marks the first time in the history of the Federal Republic of Germany that a federal law on integration has been passed. Its stated aim is to "make it easier for refugees to integrate into society" (Federal Government of Germany, 2016) and the act sets out both rights and responsibilities for newcomers to Germany in order to facilitate this process. It was introduced in order to tackle concerns in German society about the ability of refugees from both a different cultural and economic background to settle successfully and peacefully into their new home. Its provisions generally aim to help start the integration process earlier, with a particularly strong focus on integration into the labour market. The act also aims to facilitate access to education and training.

Some of its key features are:

1. Allowing federal states to assign refugees to a specific place of residence for the first three years. The goal is both to avoid too high a concentration of refugees in specific areas, such as urban centres, and to help them build relationships over time through staying in one geographical location.
2. Obliging refugees to take part in an integration course or face curtailment of their welfare benefits.
3. Increasing class sizes to get more people into integration courses quicker and requiring providers to publish information about their courses. The waiting times for integration classes were also reduced from three months to six weeks and their content developed to place a stronger focus on communicating values important in German society.
4. Making young asylum seekers with a good prospect of staying and recognised refugees eligible for grants to facilitate attendance at vocational training courses.
5. Granting exceptional leave to remain to trainees while they undergo vocational training. Those taken on as employees by the training enterprise will then be given a two-year right of residency.
6. Giving asylum seekers permission to reside once they've been issued with an arrival certificate; this should provide legal certainty and facilitate earlier access to integration courses and the labour market.
7. Providing settlement permits only to those recognised refugees who have shown a willingness to integrate.

On access to the labour market, the act:

1. Created a jobs programme called Refugee Integration Measures, which aims to create opportunities for work for asylum seekers awaiting the outcome of their applications. This involves low-paid or workfare jobs which can, for example, take place within the refugee shelters, such as serving meals or tending to green spaces.

2. Suspends the need for the labour market priority check by the Federal Employment Agency for three years, with some caveats.

(Federal Government, 2016)

The act was broadly welcomed in Germany for taking concerted action to address integration issues. It also helped to deal with a backlog of the large numbers who arrived in 2015 and promoted a focus on both the rights and responsibilities of new arrivals. In interviews in Berlin for this publication, the staff of two SPD MPs who supported the act outlined their views. The assistant to Karamba Diaby highlighted his support for the new law based on its efforts to facilitate labour market access, as did an aide to Daniela Kolbe. However, the act has also faced some criticism for the restrictions placed on asylum seekers and refugees – a reminder about balancing control and immigrant rights – and both MPs have expressed reservations about these. Diaby's office raised concerns about allocating a specific place of residence to refugees, from which they cannot choose to leave for three years. Under this system, states can add additional direction, for example telling the refugees specifically which districts or cities they can and cannot live in. However, they also have to provide opportunities and cannot just send the refugees to "empty" areas. Kolbe has expressed reservations about actions such as withdrawing access to language classes for refugees from countries like Afghanistan. The SPD has generally tended to favour an integration approach based on rewards rather than punishment and in Germany's coalition government the party has tended to take responsibility for the 'soft' integration measures such as language courses.

Developing the act was a complex process and involved an effort to include different stakeholders, including a broader range of political actors. A representative of the Ministry of Labour and Social Affairs outlined in an interview the much greater involvement of his office in an area that would usually be the preserve of the Ministry of Interior. He welcomed in particular the suspension of the labour market test, saying its existence was something that had frustrated employers and refugees alike, but pointed out that the abolition is not absolute. The test was only abolished where the unemployment rate in that area was below the state average: he described this as a way of communicating to Germans that they would not lose their jobs to refugees. In reality, every state but Mecklenburg-Vorpommern, North Rhine-Westphalia and, in particular, Bavaria – where opposition to immigration is especially high – has now effectively abolished the test. A representative of the Federal Employment Agency stressed the importance of the consultation process in developing the act, having participated in a public hearing at the Bundestag (parliament) on the new law, answering questions on its labour market provisions.

Other legislative action has been far more controversial. The 'Asylpaket II' (Asylum Package II) was adopted in February 2016 and is seen by supporters as part of a pragmatic effort to reduce both the numbers of people in the country and their length of stay, thus relieving the systemic pressure. It also cuts the time for processing asylum applications, which at the time of its introduction could still take more than a year. Critics have pointed to its suspension of family reunification for those with subsidiary protection, as well as the issuing of temporary residence, rather than the permanent residence issued to refugees under the Refugee Convention. Perhaps its most contested element is the designation of certain countries, including Algeria, Morocco and Tunisia, as "safe", meaning that applicants from those countries are almost certain to be refused. Both pieces of legislation prioritise Syrians, who are widely seen as the main beneficiaries of the new laws, leading to some unintended consequences. Some nationalities, for example, have been excluded from accessing integration courses by the Integration Act, which has stirred hostilities towards Syrians. To help respond to such challenges, separate integration courses, run by civil society and provided to those who do not qualify for the state-sponsored ones, have been established.

SWEDEN: 21 POLICIES FROM ARRIVAL TO INTEGRATION

In response to the pressures exerted by the refugee crisis on Sweden, the government, backed by most of the opposition parties, came up with a plan for action on a set of 21 policy areas (Government Offices of Sweden, 23 October 2016). These were designed to react to the situation in a comprehensive way, from the moment newcomers arrive through to long-term integration issues. The agreement was made between the governing Social Democrats and Greens and the opposition Moderate party, Centre party, Liberals and Christian Democrats. The only party in parliament excluded was the Sweden Democrats. This forms part of a long-held strategy in which all of Sweden's mainstream parties have collaborated to isolate the far-right group. However, with the party still polling well at the end of 2016 (see for example November 2016's Aftonbladet poll; Jomshof, 2016), this may change. The Moderate MP Johan Forssell noted during an interview in Stockholm that it may have been the failure of the numerous mainstream parties to offer distinctly different programmes that drove frustrated voters to the Sweden Democrats in the first place.

The 21 measures were grouped into three broad categories, together forming a holistic action plan: those to reinforce Sweden's asylum system; those to support new arrivals in Sweden; and those to bolster resources to handle the refugee crisis. The first category focused particularly on reducing congestion in the system, with the Swedish Migration Agency required to come up with ways of reducing asylum application processing times. It was proposed that those living in Migration Agency accommodation who were subject to non-appealable refusal-of-entry orders or expulsion orders should lose their entitlement to accommodation when their deadline to leave the country passed. At the same time, those granted a residence permit should be systematically discharged and not allowed to reject an offer of allocated housing in order to remain in Migration Agency accommodation. One of the most notable, and widely criticised, changes was to move from giving permanent residence status to most refugees to providing only temporary status for refugees other than quota refugees, families with children and unaccompanied children, in a move not dissimilar to that in Germany. The new permits are granted for three years, after which there is an option to apply for permanent residence if the applicant can prove that they have an assessed income sufficient to support themselves. However, Sweden also promised to increase its reception of quota refugees and explore other options for relocating people safely, such as through humanitarian visas.

The second category of measures sought to ensure quick and effective "establishment" of immigrants, in particular in relation to the labour market, education and housing. A key decision was to make the time spent awaiting an asylum application more productive, through the provision of Swedish language tuition and a compulsory civic orientation programme made available through study associations. The shared responsibility of society for the reception of refugees was recognised, with a bill to distribute migrants more proportionally between municipalities. Given Sweden's concentration of high-skill jobs, there was a strong focus on the need to create opportunities for vocational training and work, thus allowing more options for new arrivals. Tax deductions for household work were expanded, including in the areas of gardening, ICT, and moving services, in order to help lower barriers into the labour market.

The document also set out plans to relax planning and building regulations to cope with the shortage of housing. The rental situation was also addressed, with a proposal to allow municipalities to construct housing for rent to the Migration Agency under long-term agreements (at the time of proposal, the Migration Agency could only enter into agreements for a maximum of six years). The need for more school places was highlighted, with an emphasis on allowing independent schools to receive newly arrived pupils in the same way as municipal schools. Municipal schools should also have more freedom to place asylum seekers in schools other than those in close proximity. The potential opportunity provided by qualified teachers arriving in the country as refugees was recognised early on, with calls to get them into work teaching students who speak the same language, while simultaneously validating their qualifications and providing them with supplementary education as required. Retired and student teachers were also identified as a possible resource in addressing the acute shortage of teaching staff, thereby recognising the benefits immigrants can bring to their new countries.

The final category of actions had a strong focus on financial resources. As in Germany, there was an understanding of the need to back up plans with practical funding. Sweden set out its intention to seek available funds from the EU, as well as developing both short and long-term plans for financing its range of responses to the crisis. The parties agreed to provide one-off funds to the municipalities in 2015, taking into account how many people arrived in each municipality as well as the proportion of adults and children. SEK 10bn (£878m) was earmarked for these activities, including SEK 200m (£17.6m) to be given directly to civil society organisations. With the 2016 budget having included SEK 1.85bn (£158m) support to municipalities for increased housing construction, the agreement confirmed that the funds would be distributed based on actual housing construction.

HELPING NEWCOMERS CONTRIBUTE AND FIT IN: FURTHER ACTION ON LABOUR MARKET ACCESS AND LANGUAGE CLASSES IN SWEDEN

Some of the greatest support for immigration arises when immigrants are perceived to be making an effort to contribute to their new society and to adapt to its customs. This requires efforts both from the host society and from newcomers, and there is increasing recognition among those seeking a more effective approach to integration across the countries examined in this study that this is a two-way street. Beyond government, others such as business and civil society, can be closely involved in this process. These examples consider how specific programmes to improve employment prospects and address language skills, both of which are at the heart of successful integration, have been developed and implemented in practice in Sweden.

'SNABBSPÅRET': MATCHING SKILLED MIGRANTS TO JOBS

'*Snabbspåret*' (the Fast Track initiative) aims to connect skilled immigrants seeking work with jobs in sectors that have skill shortages and where employers have been struggling to fill key roles. It was launched by the Swedish government in early 2015 and was targeted at people who have been granted residency permits and have work experience or education connected to a relevant sector. The programme was developed through a series of talks involving different partners. First, the government held tripartite talks in March 2015 with the social partners and the Swedish Public Employment Service (PES). These discussions identified ways of using the skills of newly arrived immigrants and matching them more quickly with the needs of industries and enterprises. Other government agencies also participated, including the National Board of Health and Welfare, the Swedish Council for Higher Education, the Swedish National Agency for Higher Vocational Education, and the Swedish Forest Agency. The government then met with organisations that had expressed an interest in creating fast tracks for their industry. These included organisations in pharmacy, tourism, health and medical care, local government, industry, health and social care, transport, painting, timber and graphics companies, real estate, energy and electronics, building, forestry and agriculture. In practical terms, the scheme has several prongs. Newly arrived immigrants can now have their foreign credentials validated in their native language rather than Swedish. Eligible immigrants are assigned a language tutor, mentor and guidance counsellor. The scheme is intended to help immigrants establish themselves in the labour market within two years (Government Offices of Sweden, 10 June 2016).

The first two initiatives were launched in December 2015. The first grew out of discussions between the PES, the Swedish Hotel and Restaurant Workers' Union, and the Swedish Hospitality industry. In this case, the partners agreed that the credentials of immigrants would be validated at the workplace using their native language. The second was focused on the healthcare sector, building on negotiations between PES, three employers' associations and seven trade unions. The city of Stockholm also has a fast-track programme for teachers, which targets qualified teachers and aims to provide them with a certificate in Swedish within two years. Intensive language training and mentoring from a qualified teacher in the immigrant's native language is provided. Further programmes have been created for professions including social scientists, social workers, chefs and butchers among others.

Fast Track has largely been welcomed by employers and trade unions, but there have also been some criticisms and setbacks. Some of those involved have warned of the importance of remembering that the government has the primary responsibility for integrating migrants, arguing that it has shown a tendency to shift its responsibility onto the social partners (Eurofound, 5 February 2016). In an interview for this publication, Liberal MP Fredrik Malm expressed reservation about the scheme, noting that some of those who participate in it are still left without work when they complete the programme. The government plans further investment in the scheme for 2017-18, in particular to support the PES.

'SVENSKUNDERVISNING FÖR INVANDRARE': BOOSTING LANGUAGE SKILLS

'Svenskundervisning för Invandrare' (Swedish for Immigrants) or SFI, is a free national language course available to all types of immigrants. To participate, one must be at least 16 years old and resident in Sweden (this is demonstrated where applicable by the holding of a residence permit). Providing a person fulfils these conditions, there is a right to the free course, guaranteed under the Education Act, with some exceptions for those who already speak Danish or Norwegian. Finnish citizens resident in Finland, but working habitually in a Swedish municipality are also eligible. The course is for beginners and teaches reading, writing and speaking the Swedish language. It is advertised as a way of progressing a person's studies or work opportunities, as well as a route to feeling part of Swedish society more quickly. Prospective learners are advised that they will develop linguistic skills to help them communicate and participate in everyday life, including at work and socialising.

The course consists of three possible paths of study (Eductus, 2017):

1. Study path 1 (SFI courses A and B): For people who have limited or no education (0–5 years) from their home country, are unable to read or write and/or are not familiar with the Latin alphabet.
2. Study path 2 (SFI courses B and C): For people who have a basic education (6–9 years) from their home country.
3. Study path 3 (SFI courses C and D): For people who have the equivalent of an upper secondary education or higher (10 years or more) from their home country.

The courses within the programme focus on situations in everyday life, which are in turn based on the Common European Framework of Reference. However, they are also adapted to the student's interests, as well as their long-term goals. The teacher and student design the course plan together at the outset. The courses are arranged and paid for by the municipality in which the participant lives. The Swedish National Agency for Education provides resources to assist SFI teachers on its website (www.skolverket.se). There is also a series of webinars available that offer ideas on how to improve the courses and better tailor them to students' needs.

Swedish for Professionals is a specific programme for skilled workers who want to learn Swedish and start working in a particular area. The programme consists of different courses related to specific areas of work. The aim of the initiative is to reduce the amount of time it takes to access the labour market and contribute to the well-being and success of immigrants through allowing them to work in the most relevant field to their training. Courses currently exist for the following professions, although there are plans to expand the number: bus drivers, entrepreneurs, craftsmen, engineers, truck drivers, educationalists, medical staff, programmers, economists, lawyers and social scientists. As with SFI, the courses are arranged and paid for by the municipalities in which the relevant students live.

The provision of language courses is a key part of Sweden's integration strategy and these courses existed prior to the refugee crisis, given that immigrants of all kinds to the country would obviously not naturally speak Swedish. The large number of refugees in 2015 created a great amount of strain on existing systems, while official courses such as SFI were not available to those who had not yet been granted asylum and thus lacked the relevant documentation. With applications still taking a year or more to process in many cases, it was seen as essential that asylum seekers had access to Swedish language courses so that their time waiting was not wasted. This gap has been filled by civil society. One organisation that has stepped in to provide classes is Studieforbunden, the Swedish Adult Education Association. In early 2015, the Swedish government put forward a proposal that study associations provide Swedish classes for asylum seekers and offered to provide SEK 30m (£2.6m) to resource it. At the time, it was hoped the amount would cover services for 20,000 people, but the demand later grew well beyond that. In August 2015, associations under the umbrella of Studieforbunden launched a range of language and social studies classes for asylum seekers under the title Swedish from Day One. They created study circles hosted in locations such as language cafés as well as opportunities to participate in social activities such as cooking and excursions around the local area. These activities took place outside the formal education system and by December 2015, 73,500 asylum seekers had participated. Further funding was subsequently granted to support the programme (Studieforbunden, 2016).

CONNECTING WITH THE PUBLIC: PROMOTING DEMOCRACY AND SOCIAL COHESION

For those nervous that immigration is happening without their consent and who harbour fears about cultural impact and security, effective communication from mainstream actors and the opportunity to have positive experiences can be helpful in assuaging concern. A notable tactic of rightwing populists has been to mobilise people around a desire to protect their identity and values and promote the message that immigrants cannot be trusted to uphold them. A range of programmes in the comparison countries have set out to promote the genuine dialogue and interaction needed in democracies in response to this attempt to drive a wedge between people from different backgrounds. These examples focus on dialogue and bringing people together rather than pushing them apart. They also highlight efforts to communicate positive progress and document and replicate best practice.

FRANCE: FRANCE TERRE D'ASILE – FOSTERING PARTNERSHIPS

The NGO *France Terre d'Asile* ("France, Land of Asylum") was founded in 1971 as a solidarity organisation whose main objective is to support asylum seekers and defend the right of asylum in France (*France Terre d'Asile*, www.france-terre-asile.org). Today, it has more than 635 employees and 350 volunteers. The organisation's primary activity is focused around the reception of asylum seekers and offering social assistance to those it comes into touch with through its centres. Over the years, its work has expanded to focus also on integration. It both advocates and contributes to public policy work, as well as developing tailored programmes for the needs of newcomers in relation to integration. In the first area, it aims to prevent the exclusion of newcomers and works in partnership with programmes whose primary focus is not on assisting migrants; in the second, it adopts a broad definition of integration and works towards helping migrants become more autonomous. The principle guiding *France Terre d'Asile*'s work is one of complementarity. Rather than replacing the role of agencies that deal with issues such as employment, it aims to supplement them. Its definition of integration is a broad one, reflecting a focus on social inclusion as well as the values and cultural norms of French society. The services begin at the reception centres when the organisation assists migrants with accessing their rights and finding housing and work. They provide a range of social and legal counselling services, in both individual and workshop formats, and walk-in services for those not staying at the centres.

The organisation has also been innovative about developing new programmes to encourage integration and understanding in both directions, particularly since the refugee crisis. One such programme is *Duos pour Demain* (Duos for Tomorrow), originally launched in Rouen in June 2014. The programme consists of establishing a relationship between a French citizen or long-term resident and a statutory refugee or other person entitled to international protection who is living in France. The goal is for the two participants to meet up regularly and for the interaction to help the refugee to learn about French society and promote both social and cultural integration. Following the publication of the famous picture of toddler Alan Kurdi in September 2015, *France Terre d'Asile* was contacted by the French Football League, who wished to finance a major project. With their support, the organisation used the model to develop a new programme called *Duos de demain*. The new initiative is billed as an exercise in solidarity and its stated objective is to assist the integration of newcomers in the following areas:

1. Improving the French language skills of those mentored through conversations, outings, lunch or dinner invitations or any initiative likely to promote cultural exchange.
2. Introducing new arrivals to their new home, planning visits to the local area (for instance, taking people to see a city's parks and

gardens, its surroundings, monuments and museums, cinema, theatre or other shows), artistic and sporting activities, as well as signposting them to more practical skills such as DIY.
3. Helping to introduce migrants to the values, history, institutions and cultural norms of French society.

Mentors must meet with their partners at least once a month over a period of six months. At the end of this period, if both parties and the relevant association agree, the mentoring can be extended by an additional six months. *France Terre d'Asile* provides coordination and also is available to intervene if problems arise during the course of the relationship. The whole relationship is entirely voluntary and can be ended at any point. An ethical charter for delivery partners, mentors and refugees exists to guide the programme. At the start of their involvement, every participant completes a questionnaire, which is then used to match each person with the most appropriate partner, using criteria such as languages spoken, professional background and personal interests.

Following the establishment of the programme, the major French trade union CFDT decided to lend its support to the programme, in particular through the provision of mentors. The UNHCR has also joined the initiative. At the time of writing, 110 mentoring relationships had been formed, and the original Rouen programme was expanding its focus onto promoting labour market integration.

Meanwhile, *France Terre d'Asile* has also consciously aimed to counter populism and anti-migrant rhetoric in some of the most challenging areas in France. This involves a consistent strategy of working in local areas, including with local media, in order to counter the perception that migrants receive more help than low-income French nationals. In a small-scale example of this effort to work against divisive messages that pit migrants against other vulnerable groups in society, the organisation selected a few cities where there was particularly strong support for the far right and developed clothes banks in these areas, seeking high-quality donations from retail stores. Instead of simply distributing clothes only to refugees or immigrants, they partnered with charities that work with people in difficult financial and social situations and brought some of their service users together with the refugees to pick out clothing. This created an opportunity for many different kinds of people to interact with one another in the clothing centres, building understanding and trust.

GERMANY: 'DEMOKRATIE LEBEN' – COUNTERING RIGHTWING EXTREMISM

Demokratie Leben (Live Democracy) is a federal programme launched in early 2015, which aims to support those committed to promoting and protecting the values of democracy, freedom and the rule of law in Germany, as they are challenged by rightwing extremists in particular (www.demokratieleben.de). It acknowledges that state and civil society must work together to respond to these threats. It is essentially a sponsorship programme for projects that aim to encourage democracy and prevent extremism. The programme was initiated under the aegis of the Federal Ministry for Family, Senior Citizens, Women and Youth. The minister, Manuela Schwesig, comes from Mecklenburg-Vorpommern, a state in the north that has long battled rightwing populism and where the AfD finished second in regional elections in September 2016. In the project outline on the ministry's website, she says her experience of extremists "bullying" villages and attacking refugees has made her "more sensitive to all forms of exclusion, devaluation and persecution" (www.demokratie-leben.de/grusswort.html).

Through the programme, the ministry supports individuals and organisations to challenge anti-democratic activities, with a focus on municipal, regional and supra-regional projects. It lists among its targets: "right-wing extremism, racism and anti-Semitism, anti-Muslim sentiment, anti-gypsyism, ultra-nationalism, homophobia, violent salafism and jihadism and leftist militancy", as well as stating its overall wish to fight what it calls "group-focused enmity". The programme was allocated €104.5 million for 2017.

Different partners are involved in the programme. There are 234 "partnerships for democracy", which can each receive up to €100,000 annual funding. These are developed by local and municipal authorities, including towns, municipalities and rural districts. They bring together decision-makers from local authorities and those involved in civil society in order to develop strategies for addressing local problems. Communities that become part of a partnership receive an "action and initiative fund", which they can use to finance specific individual measures, such as running a democracy festival or poster campaign, or producing teaching and information materials. A support committee decides which specific measures are funded with the money; this committee is comprised of representatives from the local authority, local and regional civil society activists, and members of other government institutions. A specialist coordination unit is established within an independent organisation, which is the point of contact for the local programme, oversees implementation, and publicises its work. Sponsored authorities also receive free advisory and coaching services, which are developed and provided by an office of the Federal Office for the Family and Civil Society Tasks. Publicity and communication are important elements of the programme. Sponsored municipalities receive separate additional funding for measures to promote participation, networking and publicity. A local democracy conference is organised twice a year, in which representatives from civil society, institutional representatives, and political and administrative decision-makers are invited. They then discuss the partnership's status, objectives and future work. Separate funding again is provided for youth forums which are established and run by young people, who can design and implement their own measures to promote democracy in their communities.

A further project is entitled Democracy Centres. Since 2007, the Ministry for Family Affairs in conjunction with the federal state governments has supported the development of regional advice networks to collect information and assist those affected by rightwing violence. A regional coordination centre was established in each of the 16 federal states, based either in a state ministry or an expert body. These have collected information about the expertise of both government officials and NGOs in the respective states, their work on countering rightwing extremism, racism and anti-Semitism, as well as helping victims to access services such as counselling. Under the programme, the existing regional centres will develop into 'democracy centres', further expanding their capacity in each of these areas. Each democracy centre can receive up to €620,000 per annum. As well as the major centres, the programme directly funds civil society partners. 28 NGOs working on democracy promotion or fighting rightwing extremism have been selected to receive up to €300,000 per annum each. Further funds are being made available for pilot projects: €130,000 per annum each for 96 projects focused on tackling hatred against certain groups, and the same for 44 projects which work to prevent radicalisation. The aim is to experiment with different methods and approaches which could then be replicated elsewhere if they are successful. There is a particularly strong focus on children and adolescents, as well as on developing best practice. The second group of projects are based in social settings that are considered conflict hotspots, and aim to identify constructive, democratic ways of responding. Finally, the programme includes the Live Democracy forum, which is a platform for specialist dialogue between all those involved in the programme. It provides support for specialist needs-based networking, and the exchange of knowledge between specialists participating in the federal programme. It also arranges events and expanded specialist discussions beyond the programme where required. Evaluation of the programme, which will run until 2019, is carried out by the German Youth Institute, which examines the implementation of the programme's activities, as well as their effects.

SWEDEN: 'SVERIGE TILLSAMMANS' – PROVIDING INFORMATION AND SHARING BEST PRACTICE

Sverige Tillsammans (Sweden Together) was an initiative launched by the government in 2015, aimed at improving both conditions for new arrivals in Sweden and public debate on immigration. In mid-September, the Social Democrat prime minister, Stefan Löfven, highlighted the importance of integrating newcomers as quickly and efficiently as possible, both for their own benefit and that of Sweden, which he said faced demographic challenges and needed to invest in immigrants. He also recognised that local government needed more information regarding state benefits, regulations and support from the national authorities. The initiative was billed as an exercise in national unity, which would bring together different stakeholders to get their input and ideas on how to tackle a multitude of integration issues. In practice, this meant the organisation of regional conferences across Sweden, to which a very diverse range of stakeholders were invited to discuss how best to work on the integration of newcomers. The prime minister particularly highlighted the importance of access to education and the labour market. The focus was not only on refugees, but on all newly arrived immigrants.

In spring 2016, the State Provincial Offices and county administrative boards organised 17 regional conferences across the country, allowing for the sharing of experiences and best practice, and a discussion on the challenges and opportunities presented by the reception of newcomers. All of Sweden's counties participated, as did 254 out of 290 municipalities. In total, 2,231 individuals attended the conferences. Erik Nilsson, the secretary of state to the minister for employment, Yvla Johansson, represented the government at each of the conferences. At each meeting, the relevant county government also participated (Government Offices of Sweden, 12 April 2016).

At each of the conferences, the government's policy on the reception of new arrivals, as well as how they should access employment, education, housing and health services, was presented. Further expertise was provided by representatives of the Immigration Service, Employment Agency, the National Agency for Education, Building and Planning, National Board of Health, and the Inspectorate for Health Care. Each one discussed the support they provide to local governments. Importantly, the conferences recognised that while the regions share challenges, each one also faces its own unique circumstances, and each conference was adapted to reflect this. At some meetings, there was a strong focus on the regional labour market, while others concentrated on the housing situation, and still others on education. Collaboration and cooperation was identified as one of the most important factors for creating a successful environment for integration. Organisationally, the county administrative boards took the lead on the conferences' logistics, and their work was coordinated by the County Administrative Board of Jönköping, a county in southern Sweden.

The government explicitly directed that the project should include a strong communications focus in order to increase the impact of the regional conferences and facilitate dialogue between the participants. Key discussions were recorded and broadcast on the government website as well as a press conference held at every regional conference. Media were invited to press conferences. Journalists were, however, not allowed to attend the conferences themselves for fear of their presence stifling dialogue. A hashtag #sverigetillsammans was associated with the event, generating coverage on social media.

A formal evaluation of the initiative was carried out by the County Administrative Board of Jönköping, describing the results of the conferences from both the perspective of the organisers and the participants. The organisers were pleased with the high-level participation, reporting appreciation that government officials had come out to municipalities and counties. They particularly welcomed the participation of the state secretary, saying that receiving information directly from the ministry helped to create confidence, and that his knowledge and commitment was of great importance to the conferences. It was also valuable that the municipalities had an opportunity to meet and to receive the same information. Taking both a broad national perspective and a more county-specific approach alongside each other was considered useful. Organisers further reported that the conferences helped draw attention to the refugee issue and to send a signal that this policy area was a priority for the government. The focus on multiple stakeholders was welcomed, with opportunities for national authorities to increase cooperation with other agencies and organisations. Some shortcomings were also identified. The biggest one was that not enough time had been left for discussion and questions on the official presentations. There was also concern that a few of the national-level speakers were not properly prepared, as well as a number of typical events organisation concerns for example around scheduling (Administrative County of Jönköping Evaluation, 2016).

SWEDEN: SALAR IDEAS BANK

Further initiatives in Sweden have attempted to highlight good ideas and replicate them elsewhere. A small-scale example of this is the "idea bank" created by the Swedish Association of Local Authorities and Regions (SALAR) In an interview for this publication, Lotta Dahlerus, a senior advisor at SALAR, explained that often local authorities are so busy carrying out their work they don't necessarily think to share knowledge, or may be reluctant to draw attention to themselves even for good work. The organisation therefore created a dedicated webpage on which the organisation has collated examples of best practice and effective initiatives across the municipalities and county councils in one place. It is hosted on SALAR's website and is now among the site's most popular pages. The page includes different categories for ease of reference. It features local examples of initiatives concerning employment and education; integration initiatives for children, youths, families and schools; housing and settlement; health care; municipalities and regions in their role as employers; co-operation with the civil society; and management, organisation and strategic work. The page also provides contact information for the person in charge of each municipality, who can be contacted for any follow-up information required. The page is a reasonably simple construction, but a useful tool for linking efforts around the country. The challenges in gathering the information for it are a useful reminder that good work does not always get showcased naturally and processes need to be in place to ensure information about it is spread.

NEW NARRATIVES

Progressive mainstream actors need to win back support through offering voters responses that deal with their concerns about immigration, but that transcend populist rhetoric by addressing the substantive issues in new and meaningful ways. They need to engage in debate and action on immigration, but they have choices about how they do so. That the discussion about immigration shows such similarity across time and place hints that deeper questions about public engagement and repeated patterns in political debate need to be considered too. Ordinary people have complex concerns that require more nuanced and well thought-through responses than those proffered by rightwing populist parties. The reality is that there is no simple catchall answer or one correct way of dealing with immigration, and the mainstream response to a populist challenge should not be to pretend that there is. Responding to the rise of the far right's use of immigration as a platform requires mainstream parties to go far enough to act on the issue that people are reassured and that they remain relevant, but not so far that they become indistinguishable from their challengers.

In responding, it is essential to acknowledge that both words and actions are required. Too many people feel they are not listened to, but listening alone is not enough. The construction of any kind of new narratives around immigration must also be backed up by concrete policy action, in ways that are meaningful to real people. Mainstream parties need to act and be seen to be acting, but they are also going to need the assistance and input of others with experience and expertise in this area. The range of examples outlined in the previous chapter highlights that there are many ways in which government, mainstream parties and other actors can go about intervening on these issues. A better conversation on immigration, as well as the management of integration and diversity, is a project not for one government or one party, but for the whole of society.

For the UK, the way the conversation and action now proceeds as Brexit nears is not pre-determined. While some may wish to close the door on immigration, it is up to progressives not to close the door on ideas, and many possibilities are open to those willing to consider lessons from abroad. The UK obviously cannot seek to simply copy these, but they can help guide the country forward. All the comparison countries, states with both rich and sometimes dark histories, are grappling with similar issues. In every country, there are ideas about 'good' and 'bad' immigrants and similar language is used to denote them accordingly and portray them in media. Each society faces questions of identity, integration and the balance of rights and responsibilities of different groups. This chapter considers what principles can be identified and lessons drawn for progressives from an overall consideration of the data and examples in this book. It then offers specific recommendations to UK actors, including government, regulators, civil society and business. It recognises the need for British cooperation with Europe outside the EU, and acknowledges emerging and ongoing positive examples from the UK, which should be recognised, welcomed and built upon.

PRINCIPLES

Reclaim Language and Identity Politics

Building a narrative begins with language. It matters how we talk about immigration in our politics, in our media and in casual conversation. One of the major differences between the UK and the comparison countries is that a negative attitude to immigration in the UK has shown up persistently for many years, while in other countries it has spiked more recently. Yet the negative language used to describe immigration and its extent is similar and is consistently one of the major challenges progressives face. It was raised again and again during the research for this project, by both political actors and those involved in civil society. We need to recognise that the language we use to talk about immigration is a choice and then choose wisely.

Both German and Swedish actors have displayed efforts to challenge divisive language and replace it with more positive wording. A number of SPD representatives in Berlin outlined their approach, as a party and personally, consciously trying to use more 'open' words. An advisor to German MP Karamba Diaby noted that he specifically aims to avoid using populist terminology. The effort is also conscious among civil society, with several groups now choosing to describe themselves as "New Germans" or "New German organisations", which are open about being united by similar beliefs and values, rather than by ethnicity or religion. Merkel's "Wir schaffen das" (roughly translated as "we can do it") was an early example of an effort by the progressive mainstream to frame the conversation in more positive terms – a narrative around the capability of Germany as a country. Though that specific slogan has since been derided, the principle is still worthwhile. As the failure of the remain campaign shows, silence does not suffice and the promotion of division must be challenged with specific alternatives.

As well as being positive, the language must speak to ordinary people. Progressives do not need to shy away from emotional language. Instead, they should start viewing emotion as a tool to establish meaningful connections. Mainstream politicians will continue struggling to win over supporters if they fail to speak to ordinary people in their terms, retaining the language and the image of a distant, technocratic elite. Progressives need to prevent the co-option of the language of democracy, rights and protection by the far right to serve their own ends, by offering their own opportunities for voters to connect and engage with them. Populist parties by their very definition claim to truly represent 'the people', but in reality the far right shows very little concern for large swathes of the population.

Related to the use of language is the way in which identity is presented. It seems clearer than ever that identity matters to people, whoever and wherever they are. For someone unmoved by nationalism, it is easy to dismiss patriotic pride as racism. Yet in the UK, that same person may feel a part of their identity was snatched by the leave vote. This is as much an example of identity politics as the feelings of a Ukip supporter. There is now some recognition that it is acceptable to be proud of your national identity, especially if that identity is English, and that it is unfair to ask people to respect the culture of every group except the white majority. People should not be asked to completely abandon their traditions and beliefs. This does not at all detract from the need to oppose any attempt to restrict minority rights. Progressives should therefore be seeking to create a society in which all of these identities can co-exist. This, in turn, is one in which diverse identities are also bound together by an inclusive narrative on identity, which recognises the trade-offs necessary to achieve this.

There are good and bad ways to go about delineating identity. It is essential that the mainstream does not leave the field of identity politics to those who couch it only in negative terms about what 'we' are not. It is common for liberals to prefer a sense of identity that focuses not on where you are born, but on what you believe and the respect you are prepared to show for others. However, the ability to make this appeal to some groups may be limited. Nationalism comes in different forms and the damaging ethno-nationalism of the far right does not have to be the only option. Ultimately, a successful British society that is both proud of its roots and open to the world may have to find a way to accommodate both a more positive nationalism and a globalist approach.

Government Should Provide Central Leadership But Involve Stakeholders

One of the most difficult challenges in an interconnected world is addressing the fact that globalisation necessitates strong, centralised leadership and coordinated policy, but democracy demands extensive involvement of ordinary people. This is reflected in the challenge of "responsible versus responsive" government identified by Peter Mair (2009). It is not easy, but also not impossible, to reconcile these demands and to create a system in which central government takes responsibility for overall leadership, but then devolves powers and includes stakeholders in a way that recognises the need for their input and continued engagement. Already multiple forces, political and non-political, are involved in the process of influencing what happens on immigration. Better understanding, utilising and reconciling them should lead to more harmonious and effective approaches. A more unified approach is required in the face of the divisions focused on by rightwing populist parties. Progressives should seek to engage different stakeholders in dialogue, build partnerships between them, share best practice and ensure that adequate funding for programmes is provided and properly distributed.

Again and again during the research for this publication, the role of local level actors, including local government, NGOs and civil society, was raised particularly when it came to handling large or sudden intakes of immigrants and action on integration. Providing opportunities for people to interact with those from different backgrounds in comfortable settings can help challenge ideas – such as the suggestion that there are 'no-go' areas in particular cities or towns – promoted by the far right. Often it is the small scale, positive stories of immigrant and refugee integration that get lost among the sensationalism of the national press, and these local level interactions give people an opportunity to see a different reality up close. In an interview for this publication, Dr Annette Tabbara, chief of staff to the minister of state to the federal chancellor and commissioner for migration, refugees and integration, explained the focus of the office's work. On integration work, it often directs its most earnest attention towards the states having the most difficulty with immigration and integration issues in the parts of Germany where public support for the far right is highest.

Connections sometimes need to be built between ministries and departments as well as central and local actors. In a Berlin interview, an advisor from the Federal Ministry of Labour and Social Affairs in Germany explained that in response to the refugee crisis, ad hoc working groups were created, including one in that heads of federal states and ministries would convene regularly to discuss the issues of the moment. A truly inclusive approach must also seek representation from immigrant voices in shaping the policies that affect them.

Approach Immigration and Integration Strategically

Dissent is part of a healthy democracy and in a democracy one needs to sell ideas and find room to engage with people who think differently. Progressives must be ready to do this as well as having a plan for implementation. There is still public goodwill present on the subject of immigration and, with the right strategy, it can be harnessed. Ipsos MORI's 2016 Global Advisor poll showed that 45 per cent of the British public *did* recognise that immigration is good for the economy. Though not as high as might be hoped, it was nonetheless sharply up from the figure of 27 per cent recorded in a similar poll in 2011, and perhaps illustrates some counterbalance to the fears outlined in Chapter 2. British Future (Katwala et al, 2014) has previously carried out work that identified half the British public as falling into a "moderate majority" or "anxious middle" who were not polarised on either end of the immigration debate, but whose positions actually depend on the reassurances and policies offered. The divisions stirred by the referendum and the refugee crisis have heightened the urgency of reaching such people. If rightwing populists can activate the idea of links between certain groups of immigrants and particular threats, an informed and motivated progressive mainstream should be able to work on improving links between immigration and positive outcomes in the public's mind.

This work begins with considering legitimate concerns about immigration and integration in a constructive way. It is true that it is not racist to talk about immigration per se, but as discussed, there are good and bad ways of doing this. A recognition that that the costs and benefits of immigration can be unevenly distributed is important, as is a wider strategy to address a shortage of resources such as in the area of housing, rather than simply scapegoating. The focus countries that took in large numbers of refugees have recently directed most of their resources towards their needs, but they also face and deal with other challenges such as those affecting second and third generation immigrants. An effective approach to dealing with immigration and integration would consider the needs and desires of established residents, those of immigrant origin and more recent arrivals, not leaving any group behind.

In the UK interviews for this publication, a repeatedly expressed concern was the lack of an integration strategy in the country and there was an emphasis on the fact that integration is a two-way process that requires action not only from immigrants, but also from the government and wider society. Many people in the UK from immigrant backgrounds or heritage face crucial challenges that may prevent them from fulfilling their potential. Any integration approach will fail if it does not address the structural inequalities and discrimination faced by minorities including Muslims, which have often existed for decades and continue to the present day. A recent report by the House of Commons Women and Equalities Committee (2016) found that Muslims face the "greatest economic disadvantages of any group in society" (with an unemployment rate of 12.8 per cent compared to 5.4 per cent for the general population. Similar trends are evident in France, where they have possibly led to some individuals taking refuge in religious identity and detaching from wider society. OECD (2015) research has found that difficulties with accessing education and work have knock-on effects on integration, leading to higher relative poverty rates and concentration in poorer-quality housing among immigrant populations.

There is a need to involve communities in efforts to promote social integration through a pragmatic approach to problems and interaction at a local level. This could involve working with people not only through the most obvious sites of integration in the workplace, schools and residential areas, but also exploring new sites for interaction (Cherti and McNeil, 2012). A number of European countries have introduced integration courses, but these could be better framed not simply as an obligation, but an opportunity for participants. A part of these classes could include bringing together groups that might normally only mix in hostile circumstances, such as those of minority backgrounds and local police. In Germany, there is recognition of the innovative potential of immigrants, as well as a conscious effort and cooperation by official bodies such as the Federal Office for Migration and Refugees and the Federal Employment Agency to address their needs. These offices have developed the 'Ankommen' app for all newcomers to Germany, helping them access relevant services and providing a beginner's language course. The REDI school of digital integration in Berlin teaches coding to refugees and supported the development of the 'Bureaucrazy' app, helping newcomers understand and navigate Germany's complex laws and procedures.

Where responsibility is allocated to stakeholders or where they offer support or services, it is also essential that this is adequately financed. Extra responsibility and pressures without sufficient resources will only fuel further anger. Last year it was agreed in Germany that the 16 federal states would receive €7bn over a three year period (2016–18) specifically to use on integration activities. In September 2015, it was announced that Swedish municipalities were to be allocated an extra SEK 41,000 (£3,600) per refugee. In April 2016, an extra SEK 10bn (£878m) per year was allocated to the municipalities for welfare services, of which they are the primary provider (European commission, July 2016).

COMMUNICATE CLEARLY, EFFECTIVELY AND TRANSPARENTLY

An essential point, and one that progressives sometimes struggle with, is that for good policy to affect public opinion positively, people need both to see that it is happening and believe that it is working. Perception matters. The net migration target was so disastrous not simply because of the actual numbers, but because the government set itself up for failure by its own standards. The UK could have had similar migration figures and a very different public reaction had expectations been better managed. There is a need for much better communication about what is going on with immigration and presenting the same information in different ways can have markedly different effects.

In Germany and Sweden, there is a strong focus among the mainstream on streamlining and making immigration routes into the country more transparent. One response to this was the trial of a points-based programme called Puma in the German state of Baden-Württemberg. In France, a multi-annual permit system has been developed, which allows for longer-term stays without non-EU immigrants having to reapply every year. While these specific approaches might not suit the UK, the transparent management of immigration routes to the country post-Brexit would be beneficial. The clearer all the available entry routes into the country are, the more secure people will feel.

Formulating good communications also means reconsidering the role of evidence and of messengers in the debate. Excessive use of statistics and economic arguments has been shown to harden the debate and myth-busting campaigns frequently do more harm than good (British Future, 2014). This does not mean a need to abandon the facts completely, but a more cautious approach would be wise, particularly as part of a broader approach that connects with people's own experiences. A 2016 British study (Rolfe et al) explored the use of video communication as a method of transmitting information, and found that facts and figures are best used to answer specific questions posed by those unsure where they stand on immigration. In Germany, information campaigns to combat false and misleading statistics have been effective according to the office of the commissioner for migration, refugees and integration, which, for example, produced a booklet entitled Germany: Country of Immigration in 2015, providing basic information about integration and refugees in response to the crisis and proving one of its most successful publications ever. All this suggests the potential for exploring new ways of using evidence. In doing so, progressives might also consider how to deliver information about immigration through new channels. Recent research by the London School of Economics (Hobolt et al 2016) reveals that members of the public may distrust politicians, but place great weight on importance of information they receive from "people like them".

RECOMMENDATIONS

With the above principles in mind, what concrete measures can specific actors in the UK adopt to move forward on dealing with immigration in a post-Brexit world?

Actions for Government

The British government needs to provide national leadership in the area of immigration and integration policy, while recognising that there must also be a real and significant role for local government. The Migrant Impact Fund, scrapped in 2010, has now made a reappearance, this time as the Controlling Migration Fund. The recognition of the need to reinstate this fund is positive, but both the amount made available and the way in which funds such as this are approached also matter. The Controlling Migration Fund contains £140m for distribution over four years, is controlled by the Home Office and is billed as a resource for "mitigating the impacts of immigration on local communities" (DCLG, Home Office, 2016). Of the total amount however, £100m is directed towards addressing immigration's impact on local services, while the remainder is targeted at "enforcement action" against illegal immigrants. Such a small pot of money, with almost one-third dedicated to enforcement rather than supporting services, risks vastly under-supporting local councils. Although illegal immigration is unpopular, the focus it receives is disproportionate. Channelling so much of an already small pot towards it risks ignoring the pressures that would persist even if Britain saw only legal immigration and indeed ignores the pressure that comes from the domestic population itself. In Germany and Sweden, increased funding has been made available to local authorities to cope with immigration. Vastly greater funding is likely to be needed by local government in the UK if it is to tackle these issues and if central government is to build better relationships with councils.

In terms of setting future immigration policy and controlling legal flows, the ongoing devolution agenda offers an opportunity with respect to establishing a greater sense of control for parts of the country that feel detached from what is going in London and especially in Westminster. Brexit could present an opportunity for more regional control over immigration depending on an area's needs and wants, which could help tackle concerns about the pace of change among other things. How to blend the development of new immigration policy into this agenda should be a significant area of focus.

On integration, more localised policy and decision-making would also make sense. Areas with high concern but little actual immigration versus those that are becoming 'super-diverse' clearly have different needs.[1] Areas with large and growing Muslim populations will require attention as well given the wider debate on the place of Islam in western societies. There are also particular groups of immigrants who have traditionally prospered, such as those of Chinese or Indian heritage, while others – for example, those with a Pakistani or Bangladeshi background – have faced greater challenges (Saggar, 2016). Dealing with this requires much more than a single uniform integration policy and spills over, as immigration policy does, into many other areas.

Positive steps have already been taken. In London, Sadiq Khan appointed the first ever deputy mayor for social integration, social mobility and community engagement in 2016, which might be an example new mayors in other cities could follow. More broadly, initiatives like the Social Integration Commission and the All Party Parliamentary Group (APPG) on Social Integration have explored the challenges and opportunities that arise from the UK's increasing diversity. Both have set out recommendations that could be taken up by government. The APPG, established in 2016, has taken several submissions of evidence since the Brexit vote and sought to include an increasing range of voices, for example through its consultations with local residents in places impacted by immigration, such as Boston, Lincolnshire and Halifax, West Yorkshire. This focus on including ordinary people should be welcomed. Such ideas could be taken up and broadened into discussions on what the UK's immigration policy should look like after it leaves the EU. The group's interim report, published in January 2017, draws on international experiences both in Europe and beyond, and makes the following key recommendations:

1. "Government must develop a comprehensive and proactive strategy for migrant integration.
2. Local authorities must be required to draw up and implement local integration action plans to reflect local needs.
3. Government must assess its current one-size-fits-all approach to immigration policy.
4. For new immigrants, integration should begin upon arrival in the UK.
5. More and better data on the integration of immigrants is needed.
6. Government should demonstrate strong political leadership on immigration in order to build public confidence and facilitate successful integration at the regional and local levels."

Previous Policy Network work supported by the Barrow Cadbury Trust has explored ways in which ordinary people might be given more of a voice in political decision making more broadly through participating in direct democracy initiatives (see Chwalisz, 2015). Such initiatives could provide an additional opportunity for the public to make their concerns known and propose and debate possible responses.

Any action on integration requires a focus on education and skills development, access to the labour market, and language classes for all who need them, to ensure that immigrants have the resources and opportunities they need to play a full role in British society. In exploring how to best achieve these goals, policymakers might draw inspiration from some of the examples in Chapter 3 of this publication as well as seeking out their own from other European and, indeed, non-European countries, and the growing body of comparative literature on this topic. To recap, this might include actions such as:

1. Implementing legislation that addresses specific integration issues.
2. Creating programmes to get newcomers into employment as early as possible.
3. Viewing integration as a two-way process and focusing on both rights and responsibilities of both host communities and immigrants.
4. Providing for the quick recognition of qualifications.
5. Providing profession-specific language training.
6. Liaising with civil society groups to provide services.

Central government must have a role in both taking responsibility for the successful integration of immigrants and those of immigrant origin, while also working to tackle the fears of the domestic population, including through action to address economic concerns. Continued measures should be taken to ensure the protection and enforcement of labour standards and to prevent the undercutting of wages.

Actions for Regulators

A functioning democracy requires a system of checks and balances. The UK has already proven itself robust in terms of clarifications through the legal system on the process for triggering Article 50 and for Brexit. Fortunately, the country is facing nothing like as severe an assault on its institutions as the US is under the Trump administration. Nonetheless, there are alarming signs – such as the documented rise in reported hate crimes following the Brexit vote – that might be countered in part through the better use of independent bodies' regulatory powers. Organisations operating in the public sphere could be further empowered to intervene when debate in politics, policy and campaigning veers in an overly divisive direction and indeed when individuals or organisations are breaking relevant laws. At present, both the Electoral Commission and the Equality and Human Rights Commission (EHRC) offer guidance at election time. The latter has previously issued guidance for local authorities, candidates and political parties explaining how equality and human rights law applies and operates during an election period. However, it has suffered large funding cuts in recent years, meaning its power to monitor violations and enforce compliance has been seriously limited. At the time of its creation in 2007, the EHRC had an annual budget of £70m (Government Equalities Office, 2013). For 2016–17, it was allocated just £21.435m (Parliament, 2016). While there has been an explosion of fact-checking organisations, which aim to debunk some of the myths perpetuated by the tabloid press and on social media, a stronger role for the EHRC could help deter hateful rhetoric from not only populist but also mainstream parties in the UK. To do so, it needs to be given stronger powers to intervene and provided with the resources to perform this role effectively.

Actions for Civil Society and Business

The debate about immigration often tends to be dominated both in government and national media by negative voices, as was examined in Chapter 1. There is a need to open the debate up to more voices and for the opportunities of immigration and positive stories to be heard as well as the challenging ones. Many actors outside of government have taken their own actions in countries facing a backlash against immigration. Social cohesion and the management of diversity depend on much more than just government direction or intervention. Across countries facing negative rhetoric and push-back against immigration, civil society organisations have been able to cut through some of the noise, both improving the conversation and providing valuable services, as in the case studies outlined in Chapter 3. A flourishing civil society is an important part of any democracy and as debates have become more polarised, its role has perhaps grown more important than ever. There is also a role for business and employers in reshaping the conversation and using their resources to take concerted positive action.

Civil society groups in the UK can have a positive impact on both the national conversation about, and actions taken on, immigration, integration and diversity in a number of ways. First, through continuing to create community-based initiatives that provide a forum for dialogue. These supply opportunities for people from different backgrounds to come together and learn about each other. The Visit My Mosque programme, initiated by the Muslim Council of Britain in 2015, sees mosques across the country open their doors to the public for a day. In 2017, 150 mosques participated. Such activities may help address negative stereotyping. Other programmes, like the National Citizen Service, provide opportunities for young people in particular to interact with those of different backgrounds, building understanding while also providing networking opportunities for those who may come from disadvantaged socioeconomic backgrounds. Often it is the small-scale, positive stories of immigrant and refugee integration that get lost among the sensationalism of the national press, and these local level interactions give people an opportunity to see up close a different reality. Civil society might also liaise with local media, who can play a role in reporting positive stories about immigration and immigrants relevant to local communities, and showcasing their contribution to society.

Second, civil society groups provide a forum for self-expression and the opportunity to organise to put pressure on mainstream political actors. The protests of early 2017 included many organised civil society groups, marching in defence of their shared values. As well as connecting the like-minded, they provided them with a voice when they did not feel represented by government. Civil society also allows a space for communities who have suffered, or fear, attacks rooted in racism or prejudice, to come together and feel that they have some protection and voice independent of the state. Civil society organisations can provide a voice for immigrant groups and help them organise in ways that allow them to make meaningful submissions to government processes and to publicise their stories. These groups are often well placed to gather information from immigrants themselves, for example through analysis of their casework, which they can then use as the basis for policy recommendations. They can contribute to an informed debate by publishing relevant data and holding political parties to account. The fact that many organisations, on the other hand, adopt a policy of political neutrality can be attractive to both those who do not want to sign up to support the policy agenda of a specific political party and to those who are vocal supporters of one or another party. This may present opportunities for people to interact with their opponents in a de-politicised space, as well as providing a welcome environment for people who may know little about the political discussion, or who may simply prefer not to engage in it.

Third, civil society organisations can provide valuable services, especially for vulnerable members of society, as well as filling gaps while new policies are being developed. Civil society may be able to help deliver integration initiatives and implement programmes such as language classes. It can also perform outreach into particular communities to encourage individuals to come forward and seek assistance or join classes, where government or figures of authority may not be able to establish the trust or connections to do so. A more adequately resourced migration fund could include a dedicated local funding mechanism for the voluntary sector.

Beyond civil society, business and employers are some of the strongest voices in favour of immigration. While some claim this support is driven by a desire for the supply of cheap labour, the strict enforcement of labour and wage standards should counter such criticisms. Many businesses recruit highly skilled workers and they have been able to influence policy positively in their favour in the past. The direction of debate and policy development on immigration is of particular interest, for example, to the City of London and to the tech sector. This might allow progressives to form alliances with groups and sectors of society with whom they may not traditionally have worked closely. We no longer have a clear divide of a party of business on the right and a party of the workers on the left, nor are voters divided firmly along those lines. It thus makes sense for progressives to reach across what were once classic divides and establish new partnerships. Interesting initiatives from outside of Europe, such as the drive by Starbucks to hire refugees in the US, provide examples of how business can make a powerful statement as well as offering practical opportunities.

Cooperating with Europe

Determining the nature of the UK's relationship with Europe outside of the EU will plainly be difficult. Yet no matter how hard the Brexit, the country will have to continue to co-operate with its neighbours on a whole range of issues, which include security and elements of the management of borders. Co-operation will continue to be required for the joint management of Dover and Calais, while the future of the Northern Irish border outside of not just the EU, but also the customs union is unclear. These truths, glossed over during the referendum campaign, are now unavoidable realities. On top of this, there is still potential for the creation of more border issues in the future, for example if Scotland were to vote for independence in any second referendum. As such, the UK should seek to work as effectively as it can with European countries and the EU as a bloc. The sharing of intelligence and expertise is in everybody's interest.

NOTES

1. Parts of the UK that can be considered 'super-diverse' are those where white British are outnumbered by ethnic minorities (such as in Leicester, Slough and Luton).

CONCLUSION

International migration is an inevitable product of a modern, globalised world, where economies are interlinked, opportunities vary and travel is possible, and many people face instability and conflict in their countries of origin. In the 20th century, economic, political and technological shifts increased the capacity and motive for movement across international borders, and many European states moved from being countries of emigration to being countries of immigration. Since the turn of the century, these trends have intensified and those countries have been grappling with the challenges and opportunities immigration brings to their societies.

As things have changed, public consciousness of immigration has risen and anxiety has set in. Fear of change is natural, but the intensity of the anxiety immigration has recently produced in the UK and Europe is not. Rightwing populist parties have been leading the charge against immigration, presenting a picture of a divided and dangerous world, in which those from different national backgrounds are inevitably in conflict with one another. And yet, at the same time the refugee crisis was unfolding, extensive international progress was also being made. The UN adopted the sustainable development goals in September 2015 and the Paris climate agreement just three months later. Overall, the world today is a safer and more prosperous place than it has ever been. There are difficult global challenges ahead, but the capacity exists to fight them, if we work together.

Trust in mainstream political parties was deeply damaged by past mistakes, including those of the financial crisis, and rightly so. Too often, they have pushed ahead with an agenda that does not work for enough of the people they are elected to serve, and have come to seem distant, elitist and out of touch. The EU referendum and the refugee crisis provided flashpoints around which feelings of vulnerability, hostility and mistrust were crystallised, and immigration became the weapon with which the European far right was able to mount its most aggressive comeback since the end of the second world war. The influence of these parties on the conversation about immigration is the result of both populist successes and mainstream failures, for which multiple actors must take responsibility. Presenting national governments as unreliable and out of control has become easier in the face of bickering at both national and European level. Had EU member states cooperated more effectively in 2015, the refugee crisis could have been managed in a much more orderly and effective way. Had the remain campaign connected with more people, listened to and addressed their fears, we might be facing a very different political reality in the UK today.

To advance towards a more productive conversation on immigration, progressives must step up and acknowledge past mistakes, including their own, and seek out better solutions. The patterns of negative messaging, which we see repeated over time and in different contexts, belie the idea that concern about immigration in the UK can be dealt with only by reducing numbers, ending free movement or closing the door on refugees. It is time for a reconsideration of the way the debate about immigration is conducted, how connections are made and options are put on the table. With the advent of Brexit, the chance to blame the EU for the UK's immigration challenges will fall away and something more constructive will have to be put in its place.

The evidence, principles and recommendations put forth in this book offer some guidance as to what direction a new approach to immigration in public and political debate might take. A key component of a progressive response must be solidarity and a willingness to share and learn from one another. The analysis in this publication is a snapshot of a much bigger story in which politicians, academics, civil society, members of the public and many more actors are coming together to develop capability and knowledge to respond both to the reality of immigration and to the myths and perceptions that surround it. If this momentum can be harnessed and these ideas developed, then the tumult we are now seeing could yet give way to a more positive outcome on immigration.

REFERENCES

Administrative County Board of Jönköping, Sverige tillsammans, Utvärdering av regionala konferenserna Sverige tillsammans (Sweden Together. Evaluation of regional conferences)', 2016, www.lansstyrelsen.se/integration

Allen, William and Scott Blinder, 'UK public opinion toward immigration: Overall attitudes and level of concern', *Migration Observatory*, 28 November 2016 http://www.migrationobservatory.ox.ac.uk/resources/briefings/uk-public-opinion toward-immigration-overall-attitudes-and-level-of-concern/

All Party Parliamentary Group on Social Integration, Interim Report Into the Integration of Immigrants, 2017, http://www.socialintegrationappg.org.uk/news-reportlaunch 050117

Assinder, Nick, 'Ukip and Cameron's war of words'. *BBC*, 4 April 2006, http://news.bbc.co.uk/1/hi/uk_politics/4875502.stm

Bale, Tim (2014), 'Putting it right? The Labour party's big shift on immigration since 2010'. *Political Quarterly*. 85(3): 296–303.

Bartsch, Matthias, Andrea Brandt and Daniel Steinvorth, 'Turkish immigration to Germany: A sorry history of self deception and wasted opportunities', *Spiegel*, 7 September 2010 http://www.spiegel.de/international/germany/turkish-immigration-to-germany-a sorry-history-of-self-deception-and-wasted-opportunities-a-716067.html.

Bellon, Tina, 'Anti-immigrant AfD says Muslims not welcome in Germany', *Reuters*, 1 May 2016, http://www.reuters.com/article/us-germany-afd-islam-idUSKCN0XS16P

Benner, Thorsten (26 September 2016), 'Germany's right-wing challenge: How Merkel should respond", *Foreign Affairs*, https://www.foreignaffairs.com/articles/2016-09 26/germanys-right-wing-challenge?cid=nlctwofa 20160929&sp_mid=52423642&sp_rid=bWdsYXZleUBwb2xpY 3ktbmV0d29yay5u XQS1&spMailingID=52423642&spUserID=MjE4 MzQ0MzcxMTM4S0&spJobID= 005052477&spReportId=MTAwNTA 1MjQ3NwS2

Benton, Meghan and Anne Nielsen, 'Integrating Europe's Muslim minorities: Public anxieties, policy responses', Migration Policy Institute, 10 May 2013, http://www.migrationpolicy.org/article/integrating-europes-muslim-minorities-public anxieties-policy-responses

Blinder, Scott (July 2016, 'Migration to the UK: Asylum', *Migration Observatory*, http://www.migrationobservatory.ox.ac.uk/resources/briefings/migration-to-the-uk asylum/

Borkert, Maren and Wolfgang Bosswick, 'Migration policy-making in Germany – between national reluctance and local pragmatism?' IMIS-COE, December 2007, http://www.migrationeducation.org/fileadmin/uploads/IMISCOE_Working_Paper_ grationpolicymakinginGermany.pdf

Bourne, Jenny (December 2015), 'How should we evaluate the Race Relations Acts fifty years on?' In *How Far Have We Come? Lessons from the 1965 Race Relations Act,* Ed Omar Khan. London: Runnymede Trust.

British Social Attitudes Survey (2014), http://www.bsa.natcen. ac.uk/latest-report/british social-attitudes-31/key-findings/britain-2014.aspx

British Social Attitudes Survey (2016), http://www.natcen.ac.uk/news-media/press releases/2016/june/big-majority-believe-immigration-increases-pressure-on-schools and-hospitals/

Camus, Renaud (2011), *Le Grand Remplacement*, France: David Reinharc.

Chadwick, Lauren, 'France's National Front finds support among Millennials', *NBC*, 24 December 2016, http://www.nbcnews.com/news/world/france-s-national-front-finds support-among-millennials-n697681

Channel 4 (2016) *What British Muslims Really Think*, London: Channel 4 http://www.channel4.com/programmes/what-british-muslims-really-think

Cherti, Myriam and Claire McNeil (2012), *Rethinking Integration*, London: Institute for Public Policy Research. http://www.ippr.org/files/images/media/files/publication/2012/10/rethinking integration_Oct2012_9761. pdf?noredirect=1

Chwalisz, Claudia (2015), *The Populist Signal: Why Politics and Democracy Need to Change*, London: Rowman and Littlefield.

Conservative Party (2005), *Time for Action*, London: Conservative Party. http://news.bbc.co.uk/1/shared/bsp/hi/pdfs/11_04_05_conservative_manifesto.pdf

Conservative Party (2010), *Invitation to Join the Government of Britain*, London: Conservative Party, http://conservativehome.blogs.com/files/conservative-manifesto 2010.pdf

Della Porta, Donatella, Manuela Caiani and Claudius Wagemann (2012), *Mobilizing on the Extreme Right: Germany, Italy, and the United States*, Oxford: University Press.

'Controlling Migration Fund: Mitigating the impacts of immigration on local communities Prospectus', Department for Communities and Local Government and Home Office, 2016, https://www.gov.uk/government/publications/controlling-migration-fund prospectus

'The Casey Review: A Review Into Opportunity and Integration', Department for Communities and Local Government, 2016, https://www.gov.uk/government/publications/the-casey-review-a-review-into opportunity-and-integration

Dustmann, Christian and Tommaso Frattini (2013), *The Fiscal Effects of Immigration to the UK*, London: Centre for Research and Analysis of Migration, Department of Economics, University College London. http://www.cream migration.org/publ_uploads/CDP_22_13.pdf

DW, 'German states to receive billions more to integrate refugees', *DW*, 7 July 2016, http://www.dw.com/en/german-states-to-receive-billions-more-to-integrate refugees/a-19387096

Eductus (2015), *Swedish for Immigrants*, https://newinsweden.eductus.se/swedish-for immigrants-sfi/

El Karoui, Hakim (2016), *Un Islam Francais est Possible*, Paris: Institut Montaigne http://www.institutmontaigne.org/res/files/publications/rapport-un-islam-francais est_-possible.pdf

'Equality and Human Rights Law during an Election Period Guidance for local authorities, candidates and political parties', Equality and Human Rights Commission, 2015, https://www.gov.uk/government/uploads/system/uploads/attachment_data/file/86430 Comprehensive_Budget_Review_of_the_EHRC_.pdf

Esipova, Neli and Anita Pugliese and Julie Ray, 'Europeans most negative toward immigration', *Gallup*, 16 October 2015, http://www.gallup.com/poll/186209/europeans-negative-toward-immigration.aspx

'Sweden: Fast-track initiative to help asylum-seekers enter labour market', Eurofound, 4 May 2016, https://www.eurofound.europa.eu/observatories/eurwork/articles/labour market-social-policies/sweden-fast-track-initiative-to-help-asylum-seekers-enter labour-market

'Social dumping', Eurofound, 19 May 2016, https://www.eurofound. europa.eu/observatories/eurwork/industrial-relations dictionary/ social-dumping-0

'Turkey: Refugee crisis ECHO Fact Sheet', European Commission. January 2017. ESPN Flash Report 2016/58. European Civil Protection and Humanitarian Aid Operations, http://ec.europa.eu/echo/files/aid/ countries/factsheets/turkey_syrian_crisis_en.pdf

'Significant increase in local welfare spending in Sweden', European Commission, July 2016.

'Autumn 2016 Standard Eurobarometer: Immigration and terrorism continue to be seen as the most important issues facing the EU', European Commission, 2016, http://europa.eu/rapid/press-release_ IP-16-4493_en.htm

Elena Fries-Tersch and Valentina Mabilia, 'Annual Report on Labour Mobility', European Commission, 2015.

'Record number of over 1.2 million first time asylum seekers registered in 2015', Eurostat, http://ec.europa.eu/eurostat/en/web/ products-press-releases/-/3-04032016-AP

'Go ahead from the Bundesrat. Integration Act to support and challenge', Federal Government of Germany, 8 July 2016, https://www. bundesregierung.de/Content/EN/Artikel/2016/07_en/2016-05-25 integrationsgesetz-beschlossen_en.html

'Bundesprogramm 2015-2019: Demokratie leben! Aktiv gegen Rechtsextremismus, Gewalt und Menschenfeindlichkeit (Living democracy! Active against rightwing extremism and violence)', Federal Ministry for Family, Senior Citizens, Women and Youth, https://www.bmfsfj.de/ blob/100330/922bb647b4c9b8154c3e77db37f2ccac/bundespr gramm-demokratie-leben-ueberblick-data.pdf

'Demokratie Leben', Federal Ministry for Family, Senior Citizens, Women and Youth, https://www.demokratie-leben.de/en/bundesprogramm/ueber-demokratieleben.html

Ford, Robert and Matthew Goodwin (2014), *Revolt on the right: Explaining Support for the Radical Right in Britain*. London: Routledge.

'Frontex launches joint Operation Triton', Frontex, 31 October 2014, http:// frontex.europa.eu/news/frontex-launches-joint-operation-triton-JSYpL7

'EU immigration to the UK', Full Fact, December 2016, https://fullfact. org/immigration/eu migration-and-uk/

Gibson, David, '"Christian" Europe without Christianity', *Huffington Post*, 11 October 2011, http://www.huffingtonpost.com/2011/08/13/a-christian-europe withou_n_924901.html

Goodhart, David, 'Accidental immigration', *Prospect*, 8 February 2010, http://www.prospectmagazine.co.uk/magazine/transforming-britain-by-accident

'Comprehensive Budget Review of the Equality and Human Rights Commission', Government Equalities Office, Department for Culture, Media and Sport, January 2013

'"Passive tolerance" of separate communities must end, says PM', Government of the UK. 18 January 2016, https://www.gov.uk/government/news/passive-tolerance-of-separate communities-must-end-says-pm

'Measures to tackle the refugee crisis', Government Offices of Sweden, 23 October 2016, http://www.government.se/4aa550/contentassets/f8effa03946941c5987f7ae76b356a 2/agreement-measures-to-tackle-the-refugee-crisis.pdf

'Fast Track – a quicker introduction of newly arrived immigrants', Government Offices of Sweden, 11 December 2015; Updated 10 June 2016, http://www.government.se/articles/2015/12/fast-track---a-quicker-introduction-of newly-arrived-immigrants/

Griffith, Phoebe, 'Theresa May must end this obsession with net migration. All migrants are not the same', *Daily Telegraph*, 20 July 2016. http://www.telegraph.co.uk/news/2016/07/20/theresa-may-must-end-this-obsession- with-net-migration-all-migra/

Hackett, Conrad, '5 facts about the Muslim population in Europe', Pew Research Center, 19 July 2016, http://www.pewresearch.org/fact-tank/2016/07/19/5-facts-about-the muslim-population-in-europe/

Haidt, Jonathan (2012), *The Righteous Mind: Why Good People are Divided by Politics and Religion*, London: Penguin UK.

Haidt, Jonathan, 'When and why nationalism beats globalism', *American Interest*, 10 July 2016, http://www.the-american-interest.com/2016/07/10/when-and-why-nationalism beats-globalism/

Hampshire, James and Tim Bale (2015), 'New administration, new immigration regime: Do parties matter after all? A UK case study', *West European Politics*, 38(1): 145-166.

Hein, Jeremy (2004), 'France: The melting pot of Europe'. In *Migration and Immigration: A Global View*, Eds Maura I. Toro-Morn and Marixsa Alicea, Connecticut: Greenwood Press.

Hobolt, Sara, Thomas J. Leeper and James Tilley, 'Voters might be fed up with politicians, but they will listen to people "like them"', *London School of Economics*, 23 June 2016, http://blogs.lse.ac.uk/europpblog/2016/06/23/voters-listen-people-like-them/

Horn, Heather, 'The voters who want Islam out of Germany'. *The Atlantic*, 27 May 2016, https://www.theatlantic.com/international/archive/2016/05/afd-germany-anti immigration/484700/

'Employment Opportunities for Muslims in the UK - Second Report of Session 2016' House of Commons Women and Equalities Committee, 17 August 2016

'The fall of Srebrenica and the failure of UN peacekeeping', Human Rights Watch, 1995, https://www.hrw.org/report/1995/10/15/fall-srebrenica-and-failure-un peacekeeping/bosnia-and-herzegovina

'Les Français et la crise des migrants en Europe', IFOP, March 2016, http://www.ifop.com/media/poll/3315-1-study_file.pdf

'The unemployment rate was stable in Q1 2016', INSEE, 19 May 2016, https://www.insee.fr/en/statistiques/2011466

Institute Montaigne, http://www.institutmontaigne.org/fr/publications/discriminations religieuses-lembauchc-une-realite#etape7

'Migrant arrivals by sea in Italy top 170,000 in 2014', International Organisation for Migration, 16 January 2015, https://www.iom.int/news/migrant-arrivals-sea-italy-top 170000-2014

'Mediterranean migrant arrivals top 363,348 in 2016; Deaths at sea: 5,079', International Organisation for Migration, 6 January 2017, https://www.iom.int/news/mediterranean-migrant-arrivals-top-363348-2016-deaths sea-5079

'Concern about immigration is at the highest level ever recorded, and continues to rise', Ipsos Mori, September 2015, https://www.ipsos mori.com/researchpublications/researcharchive/3628/EconomistIpsos-MORI September-2015-Issues-Index.aspx

'Immigration is now the top issue for voters in the EU referendum', Ipsos Mori, June 2016, https://www.ipsos-mori.com/researchpublications/researcharchive/3746/Immigration is-now-the-top-issue-for-voters-in-the-EU-referendum.aspx

'Shifting Ground. Changing Attitudes to Immigration in the Long Term and During Election Campaigns', Ipsos Mori, 2016, London: Ipsos Mori. https://www.unboundphilanthropy.org/sites/default/files/shifting-ground-attitudes-to immigration-2016.pdf

Jennings, Will and Gerry Stoker (2016), 'The bifurcation of politics: Two Englands, *Political Quarterly*, 87(3): 372–382.

Jomshof, Richard, 'Increased support for the Sweden Democrats', *Afton-baldet*, 16 November 2016, http://www.aftonbladet.se/nyheter/samhalle/article23919959.ab

Karpf, Anne, 'We've been here before', *The Guardian*, 8 June 2002, https://www.theguardian.com/uk/2002/jun/08/immigration.immigrationand publicservces

Katwala, Sunder, Steve Ballinger and Matthew Rhodes (2014), *How to Talk About Immigration*, London: British Future, http://www.britishfuture.

org/wp content/uploads/2014/11/How-To-Talk-About-Immigration-FINAL.pdf

Kaufmann, Eric, 'Trump and Brexit: why it's again NOT the economy, stupid', *London School of Economics*, 9 November 2016, http://blogs.lse.ac.uk/politicsandpolicy/trump-and-brexit-why-its-again-not-the economy-stupid/

Kitschelt, Herbert (1997), *The Radical Right in Western Europe: A Comparative Analysis*, University of Michigan Press.

Lawrence, Matthew (2016), *Future Proof. Britain in the 2020s*, London: Institute for Public Policy Research, http://www.ippr.org/files/publications/pdf/future proof_Dec2016.pdf?noredirect=1

Lipka, Michael, 'Muslims and Islam: Key findings in the U.S. and around the world', *Pew Research Center*, 22 July 2016, http://www.pewresearch.org/fact tank/2016/07/22/muslims-and-islam-key-findings-in-the-u-s-and-around-the-world/

Lyons, Kate and Gary Blight, 'Where in the world is the worst place to be a Christian?', *The Guardian*, 27 July 2015, https://www.theguardian.com/world/ng interactive/2015/jul/27/where-in-the-world-is-it-worst-place-to-be-a-christian

Mair, Peter (2009), *Representative Versus Responsible Government*, Cologne: Max Planck Institute for the Study of Societies.

Migration Observatory, *Migration to the UK: Asylum*, 20 July 2016, Oxford: Migration Observatory.

Migration Observatory, *A Decade of Immigration in the British Press*, 7 November 2016, Oxford: Migration Observatory.

Migration Watch UK (2014), 'An Assessment of the fiscal effects of immigration to the UK', https://www.migrationwatchuk.org/briefing-paper/1.37

Migration Watch UK. (2015), 'Immigration under Labour', https://www.migrationwatchuk.org/briefing-paper/355

'Admission to residence - Residence permits (statistics)', Ministry of the Interior of France, 2016, http://www.immigration.interieur.gouv.fr/Info-ressources/Donnees statistiques/Donnees-de-l-immigration-de-l-asile-et-de-l-acces-a-la-nationalite francaise/Archives/Statistiques-publiees-en-juillet-2016/L-admission-au-sejour-Les titres-de-sejour-statistiques

Mishra, Pankaj (2017), *Age of Anger: A History of the Present*, UK: Penguin Books. National Front, Manifesto 2017, Available at: http://www.frontnational.com/le-projet de-marine-le-pen/

Noack, Rick, 'Leaked document says 2,000 men allegedly assaulted 1,200 German women on New Year's Eve', *Washington Post*, 11 July 2016, https://www.washingtonpost.com/news/worldviews/wp/2016/07/10/

leaked-document   says-2000-men-allegedly-assaulted-1200-german-women-on-new-years eve/?utm_term=.231b00c2bcd3

OECD/ EU (2015), *Indicators of Immigrant Integration 2015*, Paris: OECD Publishing. http://www.oecd.org/els/mig/Indicators-of-Immigrant-Integration-2015.pdf

OECD (2016), *International Migration Outlook 2016*, Paris: OECD Publishing. http://dx.doi.org/10.1787/migr_outlook-2016-en

'May 2016 quarterly update: Figures for long-term immigration to the UK 2006-2015', Office for National Statistics (May 2016), Available at: https://www.ons.gov.uk/peoplepopulationandcommunity/populationandmigration/int rnationalmigration/bulletins/migrationstatisticsquarterlyreport/may2016

'Migration statistics quarterly report: Dec 2016', Office for National Statistics, December 2016, Available at: https://www.ons.gov.uk/peoplepopulationandcommunity/populationandmigration/int rnationalmigration/bulletins/migrationstatisticsquarterlyreport/dec2016#immigration   to-the-uk-was-650000-the-highest-estimate-recorded

'Equality and Human Rights Commission: Finance: Written question – 43266', Parliament.uk. 21 July 2016, https://www.parliament.uk/business/publications/written-questions-answers   statements/written-question/Commons/2016-07-18/43266/

Parveen, Nazia and Harriet Sherwood, 'Police log fivefold rise in race-hate complaints since Brexit result', *The Guardian*, 30 June 2016, https://www.theguardian.com/world/2016/jun/30/police-report-fivefold-increase-race -hate-crimes-since-brexit-result

Phillips, Trevor, 'What do British Muslims really think?' *The Times*, 10   April   2016,   http://www.thetimes.co.uk/article/my-sons-living-hell-j72t7fppc

Polakow-Suransky, Sasha, 'The ruthlessly effective rebranding of Europe's new far right'. *The Guardian*. 1 November 2016, https://www.theguardian.com/world/2016/nov/01/the-ruthlessly-effective-rebranding-of-europes-new-far-right

Powell, Enoch. (1968), Full text of speech available at: http://www.telegraph.co.uk/comment/3643823/Enoch-Powells-Rivers-of-Blood speech.html

'"Passive tolerance' of separate communities must end, says PM"', Prime Minister's Office, 18 January 2016, https://www.gov.uk/government/news/passive-tolerance-of separate-communities-must-end-says-pm

Rolfe, Heather, Jonathan Portes and Nathan Hudson-Sharp (February 2016), *Changing the Debate: Video Animation on the Impact of Immigration on the UK*, London: National Institute of Economic and Social Research. http://www.niesr.ac.uk/sites/default/files/files/Video%20 animation%20full%20report %20to%20CoL(3).pdf

Saggar, Shamit, (2016), 'Integration in Britain in 2016', Policy Network. http://www.policy network.net/pno_detail.aspx?ID=6169&title= Understanding-integration-in-Britain-in 2016

Saunders, Doug, 'Sweden's rape crisis isn't what it seems', *Globe and Mail*, 14 May 2016, http://www.theglobeandmail.com/opinion/swedens-rape-crisis-isnt-what-it seems/article30019623/

Simon, Patrick, *French National Identity and Integration: Who Belongs to the National Community?*, Washington D.C.: Migration Policy Institute, May 2012, http://www.migrationpolicy.org/research/ TCM-french-national-identity

SfX, http://sfx-yrke.se/eng

Somerville, Will (2007), *Immigration Under New Labour*, Bristol: Policy Press.

Stockham, Ruby, 'Five myths about public attitudes towards immigration', *Left Foot Forward*, 20 November 2014, https://leftfootforward. org/2014/11/five-myths-about public-attitudes-towards-immigration/

Studieforbunden. (2015), 'Swedish from Day 1', http://studieforbunden.se/ wp content/files/Swedish_from_day_one_ _adult_education_with_asy-lum_seekers_in_2015.pdf?2f7c15

Swales, Kirby (2016), *Understanding the Leave Vote*, London: NatCen: http://whatukthinks.org/eu/wp-content/uploads/2016/12/NatCen_Brex-planations report-FINAL-WEB2.pdf

Sweden Together, https://translate.google.co.uk/ translate?hl=en&sl=sv&u=http://www.regeringen.se/re eringens-politik/ regeringens-etableringspaket/sverigetillsammans/&prev=search

'Nearly 163,000 people sought asylum in Sweden in 2015', Swedish Migration Agency, 12 January 2016, https://www.migrationsverket.se/English/ About-the-Migration Agency/News-archive/News-archive-2016/2016-01-12-Nearly-163000-people sought-asylum-in-Sweden-in-2015.html

'Public Perceptions of the Refugee Crisis', Tent Foundation, January 2016, https://static1.squarespace.com/static/55462dd8e4b0a65de4f3a087/ t/5706891a04426 15d0606532/1460046123082/TENT_2016Jan_Coun-tryReport-GERMANY+Re contact.pdf

'Politisch inkorrekt', *The Economist*, 6 October 2016, http://www.economist.com/news/europe/21708256-right-wing-german-media-brand builds-following-politisch-inkorrekt

'Transatlantic Trends study', The German Marshall Fund of the United States (GMF), 2014, http://trends.gmfus.org/transatlantic-trends/#lightbox/0/

'Transatlantic Trends: Mobility, Migration and Immigration', The German Marshall Fund of the United States (GMF), 2014, http://trends.gmfus.org/files/2014/09/Trends_Immigration_2014_web.pdf

'Cameron refuses to apologise to Ukip', *The Guardian*, 4 April 2006, https://www.theguardian.com/politics/2006/apr/04/conservatives.uk

'Postwar Immigration', The National Archives. , http://www.nationalarchives.gov.uk/pathways/citizenship/brave_new_world/immigra ion.htm

'Prime Minister's Initiative', The National Archives, http://webarchive.nationalarchives.gov.uk/+/http:/www.dius.gov.uk/international/pmi index.html

'Press Coverage of the Refugee and Migrant Crisis in the EU: A Content Analysis of Five European Countries', UNHCR and Cardiff University. December 2015, Cardiff: Cardiff University, http://www.media-diversity.org/en/additional files/UNHCR_Cardiff_University_Report_on_ EU_Press_Migrants_Coverage_2014 5.pdf

UNHCR (2015), 'Figures at a glance'. http://www.unhcr.org/uk/figures-at-a-glance.html

UNHCR (20 June 2016), *Global Trends: Forced Displacement in 2015*. Place: UNHCR. http://www.unhcr.org/uk/statistics/unhcrstats/576408cd7/unhcr-global-trends 2015.html

United Nations (25 April 2015), 'Statement of the high commissioner on human rights'.

'Trends in international migration', United Nations Department of Economic and Social Affairs Population Division, December 2015, http://www.un.org/en/development/desa/population/migration/publications/populatio facts/docs/MigrationPopFacts20154.pdf

Versi, Miqdaad, 'What do Muslims really think? This skewed poll certainly won't tell us', *The Guardian*, 12 April 2016, https://www.theguardian.com/commentisfree/2016/apr/12/what-do-muslims-think skewed-poll-wont-tell-us

Westin, Charles. 'Sweden: Restrictive immigration policy and multiculturalism', Migration Policy Institute, 1 June 2006, http://www.migrationpolicy.org/article/sweden restrictive-immigration-policy-and-multiculturalism

Worley, Will, 'German anti-refugee MEP blames Angela Merkel for Berlin attack: 'Those are her dead!'', *The Independent*, 19 December 2016, http://www.independent.co.uk/news/world/europe/berlin-attack-angela-merkel german-mp-blames-chancellor-for-lorry-deaths-latest-a7485486.html